OUTLIERS IN LAW

BY JOHN SHUFELDT

Inquiries should be addressed to:
Outliers Publishing
Hangar 1
7332 E. Butherus Drive
Scottsdale, AZ 85260

info@ingredientsofoutliers.com

Paperback—ISBN 978-1-940288-88-8

E-Book— ISBN 978-1-940288-89-5

Cover design by paja-o@live.com

Interior production by Perfect Bound Marketing + Press, Inc.

Manuscript review by Bob Kelly of WordCrafters, Inc.

TABLE OF CONTENTS

INTRODUCTION

"The business of the law is to make sense of the confusion of what we call human life – to reduce it to order but at the same time to give it possibility, scope, even dignity."

~ *Archibald MacLeish*

Whenever I see that comment by Archibald MacLeish and get to the final word, the image that generally pops into my mind is that of retired U.S. Supreme Court Justice Sandra Day O'Connor. Appointed to the high court by President Ronald Reagan in 1981, she was its first woman justice and served for 25 years with distinction and, yes, with dignity. She retired from the Court in 2006 to care for her husband, who was seriously ill. Following her retirement, Arizona State University College of Law changed its name to the Sandra Day O'Connor College of Law.

In the interests of full disclosure, I earned my Juris Doctor degree from ASU in 2005, and currently serve as an adjunct professor there, while continuing my emergency medical practice and other pursuits. Practicing emergency medicine can be rigorous and I'd been thinking of an alternative career path, should it prove wise. This was the genesis of going to law school. I wanted to be able to help physicians navigate the legal world and I thought, "Who better than someone who speaks their language."

I still clearly remember what happened one day during my first semester; I was told the Dean wanted to speak with me. I went to her office and started by thanking her for accepting me into the school. Her response; "Well, it's always good to have a doctor around in case someone drops dead!" I started to laugh, until I realized she was actually serious! Fortunately, there were no fatalities during my time there.

MacLeish, by the way, was well qualified to comment on "the business of the law." At Harvard Law School, he'd been an editor of the *Harvard Law Review* and, after graduating, he joined a Boston law firm. Three years later, he resigned to pursue a literary career as a poet and playwright. It was a wise choice, it seems, as he went on to earn three Pulitzer Prizes, two for poetry (1933 and 1953) and one for drama (1958).

Today, "the business of the law," much like virtually every profession and industry, is in the midst of significant technology-driven changes. According to a recent report by the Forbes Legal Council, these changes have led to "greater democratization of the 'industry,' and introduced new competition and continual searching for better and more efficient ways of providing legal services."

In the following pages, you'll meet six men and women who are actively engaged in the multi-faceted business of the law. They include an entrepreneurial lawyer who's following her passion as an advocate for the families of special needs children; a professor of law, who is among the first legal scholars to focus on issues regarding online activity; a professor of law and world-renowned domestic violence activist; a veteran trial attorney specializing in medical negligence and product liability litigation; a *recent magna cum laude* law school graduate and associate intellectual property attorney with a major international law firm; and a physician and attorney who is actively involved both in business and the arts, including major film production.

J.S.

CHAPTER 1

Victoria Ames

BIOGRAPHY

"I was a teenage parent. I had my first child when I was 17. For a long time I was a very headstrong person, yet I understood that it was an overwhelming task to be in college and raising a child by myself. My father had passed away and my mother had significant health issues, so in many ways I was on my own, raising this child who ended up having a serious, life-threatening illness. That's when my passion for helping those caring for loved ones with special needs began."

~ Victoria Ames

Victoria Ames is a partner and co-owner of Artemis Law Firm in Scottsdale, Arizona. She has dedicated her career to assisting others as an advocate for the rights of those with special needs and improving the lives of families faced with caring for loved ones with special needs through her practice.

She graduated from George Mason University with a Bachelor of Science in clinical psychology and human development. Soon thereafter she completed additional classes to finish a degree in accounting and finance. She worked as an accountant and business manager for a large company in Washington, D.C. for a number of years before attending Marymount University, where she earned her Master's Degree in Psychology and Human Behavior.

Following graduation, Ames worked for the Arizona State Department of Health Services, developing and monitoring policies and practices for statewide behavioral health care. She was then hired as a Senior Regional Manager for the Make-A-Wish Foundation of America. Three years later, she was named CEO for Make-A-Wish Foundation International, where she guided the organization's international expansion efforts in more than 30 countries.

In 2006, Ames enrolled at the Sandra Day O'Connor College of Law at Arizona State University (ASU), where she earned her law degree in 2009. She wanted to combine her business and psychology background with her passion for helping families faced with special needs, so she opened the Artemis Law Firm in 2014, which has a dedicated practice area specializing in law for special needs families.

Ames also directs the Sandra Day O'Connor College of Law's Legal Services Program, which provides free legal services to those who cannot afford legal assistance.

INTERVIEW

Q: Will you please introduce yourself?

A: My name is Victoria Ames, and I'm a partner and co-owner of the Artemis Law Firm in Scottsdale, Arizona.

I did not start my career working in the law. When I was in high school, I decided to study business when I was in college, because that was my interest at that time. So, I spent four years pursuing a degree in business and finance.

But, before I graduated, I had a significant health issue with my oldest child. At age 3, he was diagnosed with a life-threatening illness, one for which there was no cure. So, I decided I needed to know more about how to help kids deal with such illnesses.

I left the business path and ended up spending a year focusing on psychology and biochemistry. Ultimately I graduated with a degree in clinical psychology and human development. It wasn't long before I realized that while this new focus gave me a lot of insight into the dynamics of children and families, I couldn't make a living at it with only a bachelor's degree.

So, I went back and took the last two classes I needed to obtain a second degree in accounting and finance. I started working for a corporation in Washington, D.C. that sold and leased computers.

While I'm grateful for the opportunity to work in accounting and finance, and learned a lot about international business and mergers and acquisitions, I realized accounting wasn't my passion or what I wanted to do long-term. It was great knowledge and I've used all of it every day since then. But, I was missing something I wanted in my life.

I returned to graduate school to pursue a Ph.D. in psychology and healthcare, because I wanted to return to helping people with significant health issues. I left the program midway with only a master's degree because my family was transferred to Phoenix, and I'd been living in Washington, D.C.

When I came to Phoenix, I began working with children and families in crisis. After working with the Arizona State Department of Health and Human Services, I landed a job at the Make-A-Wish Foundation, where I combined my skills as a business and finance professional with my passion and training in helping families and children.

There, I oversaw the chapter development division, where I did both the financial audits and business compliance audits of the U.S. chapters. I also developed and help implement the program policies nationwide.

About three years later, I transferred to Make-A-Wish Foundation International and became the CEO; it was one of the best jobs I've had until now. I was fortunate to have been promoted and to have had the opportunity to work for ten years growing the organization, and developing programs around the world to bring Make-A-Wish to more than 30 countries. It was fantastic.

Q: What made you interested in law school?

A: Somewhere along the way, I realized how important it was to understand the impact of the law on both families and the businesses established to serve them. I thought, "Maybe this is something I should pursue." Then, one day when I was in the midst of a discussion about contract compliance with a colleague, I asked for an explanation of his reasoning on a particular item. He said, "Well, I'd explain it to you but you're not a lawyer, so you wouldn't understand." Enough said.

That was the beginning of my road to lawyering. I graduated from law school in 2009.

I'm still in the early stages of my legal career, but I can tell you that the 20 years of experience I had before becoming a lawyer have added more to my understanding of lawyering and my ability to be a lawyer than 20 years without that experience could ever have brought me. I'm grateful for that every day.

I didn't at all feel intimidated or frightened by the thought of returning to school; I was excited by the opportunity. That's one of the biggest things I've learned over the years – embrace change. When I was 20, unexpected happenings gave me pause and made me contemplate whether or not I was ready to take on that particular challenge, or whether or not I wanted to face that unknown.

But now, after what I've experienced and learned, I view every new opportunity as an exciting prospect. If it works, that's fantastic. If it doesn't work, I know I've gained something from the experience, and that's pretty fantastic too.

I don't feel frightened, disillusioned or disappointed much anymore. At this stage I feel everything has some kind of a positive impact, whether it's the one I hoped it would be or something surprising. In the end, each event contributes in a positive way to who I am as a human being and how I fit into the world around me. I try to remain optimistic in that way and be thankful even for the small things.

Q: Would you say working with children and families was your passion?

A: Well, yes, it's certainly something I'm passionate about; especially helping children and families who have significant health and psychological issues. We all have a lot of stressors in our lives. It makes me feel good to do what I can to alleviate that as much as possible for people who aren't in a position to do it on their own.

I was a teenage parent; I had my first child when I was 17. Even though I was headstrong, I understood what an overwhelming task it would be to be in college and raise a child by myself. My father had passed away when I was very young and my mother had suffered a stroke when I was in high school, so in many ways I was on my own, raising this child who was diagnosed with a serious, life-threatening illness. That's when my passion for helping those caring for loved ones with special needs began.

The prospect of taking on something like going to law school or medical school while raising a very sick child felt overwhelming in my early years. But as my career progressed and became successful, and I built more confidence, my resilience and determination to take on new challenges grew too.

Q: Were your friends and family supportive?

A: I've been lucky in many ways, because for the most part virtually everyone I know, both friends and family, have been supportive of the educational endeavors I've undertaken. They've been universally optimistic and supportive of things I've accomplished and positive about feeling those accomplishments would work out well for me. So, I've never had a reason to doubt myself or my pursuits in that way.

That has been an enormously positive influence for me. I've never had to second guess myself, at least when it comes to my career choices.

But, there are a lot of things I had to go through on my own. While everyone was supportive about me getting an education and pursuing a positive career, few were willing to help with my son, help pay the mounting expenses, or even let me live with them while I struggled through it. I had to figure that out on my own.

I was told, "We love you and that you're making good decisions now, but you made your bed and you're going to have to lie in it. You're going to have to accept all those responsibilities you had no business getting yourself into. So, figure it out on your own." So I did.

It wasn't until I had proved myself a number of times over before I started gaining some of that acceptance and support in the other areas of my life back. People were more than happy to show up to graduations and congratulate me for good grades, successes achieved, but helping out in other areas of my life wasn't something I had much support in. That was hurtful and hard and difficult to overcome. I wouldn't recommend it for anyone.

I would love to go back to the doubters and say, "You should never discourage a person who's trying to succeed, because it does happen." I'd love for them to recognize, 20 or 30 years later, here's the person you thought wouldn't overcome the odds.

Q: Would you say you overcame adversity?

A: It was never something I felt was a choice. Of course I had to succeed, and of course I had to overcome. I don't know that I ever believed I had an option of not making it work; the only issue was how I was going to make it work. It never occurred to me that I could give up or give in. Even now it feels foreign to contemplate that notion.

In the end, you simply have to deal with whatever comes your way. Of course, how you deal with such things is a choice, and that will define how happy and successful you ultimately are. But, because you have complete control over that part only, all you can do is choose your best path.

I don't have control over what people think about me, or whether they're going to help me, support my decisions, or whether they're going to like me. But, I have absolute control over how I'm going to deal with those things. Maybe that means simply doing everything

I can to make the most positive choices, even when faced with bad options.

Every human being has what he or she needs inside to succeed and be happy. But, for some people that inner strength is hard to find. For some, it shines openly and for others it's a hidden treasure they need to seek out.

Some people need a lot of help finding that hidden treasure that lies within them; being surrounded by people who help you find it and continually remind you it's there is invaluable.

Q: What's been your greatest success or accomplishment?

A: Having and raising my kids is the best thing I've ever done. But, from a career perspective, starting my law firm has probably been the most exciting thing I've done. Obviously there are a lot of things we accomplish in life; surviving the teenage years with a child rates pretty high; having wonderful kids despite the challenges of teenage parenthood also ranks up there. But, from a career perspective, starting a law firm that focused on things I felt strongly about has been my greatest accomplishment, and it's been the most exciting thing I've done.

When I first graduated from law school and began my career, I joined a big firm doing commercial litigation, because that's what I was told people on the right legal track did. You graduate from law school, clerk at a court, go to a big firm and do some challenging legal work, and along the way you learn about being a lawyer.

But, starting my own firm has allowed me to refocus on the same passion I've carried throughout my career pursuits – corporate, healthcare, not-for-profit, and now law.

I'm back to focusing my life on helping people who are caring for loved ones with special needs. So, my law firm has an entire practice area dedicated to helping children and adults faced with healthcare concerns, mental health stresses, substance abuse issues, traumatic brain injuries, and other challenges. The most vulnerable among us often have the least ability to secure the help they need.

Q: Are there a lot of lawyers in the special needs field?

A: My experience has been that most lawyers in the community don't work in the special needs area because there is very little money in serving that population. And, it takes a significant amount of understanding about other areas that most lawyers simply are not trained in.

I'm fortunate and delighted to be able to do what I've always enjoyed, helping people who are struggling because they don't have the support necessary in their time of greatest need. The fact that I can make even a slight difference through my work means I've accomplished something worthwhile.

Q: What's been your greatest failure or miscalculation?

A: With respect to being a lawyer, it was believing what so many claimed: that being a really good lawyer meant focusing purely on legal knowledge.

Actually, to be a really good lawyer you certainly need to know the law, but by itself it's not enough. What really makes a difference, as has been my experience throughout my career, is bringing together knowledge, experience, connections, and community resources to make a real difference.

None of us can do it on our own. I can be the best legal analyst in the world, but if my client needs some atypical service, special accommodation, or scarce resources, those aren't things I can provide on my own.

Q: What makes you happier, the pursuit of becoming a lawyer or actually being one?

A: It's all a pursuit. It's called the practice of law because you're always practicing, pursuing, perfecting. It's like the saying – "Life is a journey; not a destination." Every day is an opportunity for something new.

While I love what I'm doing now, I can't promise that in ten years I won't be doing something else, because something may come along that will provide a different opportunity. Hopefully, I'll continue to build on the passions I have, regardless of what the future brings. Quite frankly, I'm okay with that.

Q: Are you proud of the person you've become?

A: Most days, yes; but, there's always room for improvement. I'm proud of what I've achieved despite some adversity. Still, I feel there's so much more to do.

As long as I can pursue positive endeavors, whatever happens is okay. Even failing is okay.

ACTION GUIDE

An easy reference guide to the advice and tips provided by Victoria Ames

1) You Have More Control Than You Think

I don't have control over what people think about me, or whether they're going to help me, support my decisions, or whether they're going to like me. But, I have absolute control over how I'm going to deal with those things. Maybe that means simply doing everything I can to make the most positive choices, even when faced with bad options.

2) It's More Than Just the Law

To be a really good lawyer you certainly need to know the law, but by itself it's not enough. What really makes a difference, as has been my experience throughout my career, is bringing together knowledge, experience, connections, and community resources to make a real difference.

3) Stay True to Yourself, Your Values

One of the temptations I face when I'm feeling less confident about something is to do it the way someone else wants it done, simply so he or she will accept it. That generally ends badly, and then I end up missing the opportunity to pursue my own path and passions. Don't do that. Stick with your own course because ultimately that's going to be what invigorates you and keeps you happy.

4) Never, Ever Stoop

People often look for the easy way out, or the path of least resistance. They'll say, "I know this isn't the best decision, but let's just do it like this and get it over with."

Or they'll say, "If they can break the rules, so can I." My response to that is never, ever, ever engage in that. It simply isn't worth it in the end. Your integrity is everything; never jeopardize it. No matter how hard you work, no matter how many friends you've made, no matter how much knowledge, wealth, or accolades you've gained, at some point in your lifetime, rightly or wrongly, someone will challenge or question something you have done, perhaps with potentially serious consequences. At that moment, that fact that you're known to have unwavering integrity will be your salvation.

5) "Practice" Law

It's called the practice of law because you're always practicing, pursuing, perfecting. It's like the saying – "Life is a journey, not a destination." Every day is an opportunity for something new.

CHAPTER 2

Paul Schiff Berman

BIOGRAPHY

"I had a sense from popular culture that lawyers can help effectuate real change in the world. You think about the famous legal cases from history and even less well-known cases where real change happens at a large societal level because of law. And even just in an ordinary case, if a lawyer represents someone it empowers the client and could change lives, too."

~ Paul Berman

Paul Schiff Berman, Walter S. Cox Professor of Law, is one of the world's foremost theorists on the effect of globalization on the interactions among legal systems. He is the author of nearly sixty scholarly works, including Global Legal Pluralism: A Jurisprudence of Law Beyond Borders, published by Cambridge University Press in 2012. He was also among the first legal scholars to focus on legal issues regarding online activity, and is co-author of one of the leading casebooks in the field.

In addition to his scholarly work, Berman has extensive experience in university and law school administration, having served as Vice

Provost for Online Education and Academic Innovation at The George Washington University from 2013-16; Dean of The George Washington University Law School from 2011-13; and Dean of the Sandra Day O'Connor College of Law at Arizona State University from 2008-11. He previously served as a Visiting Professor and Visiting Research Scholar at Princeton University from 2005-06 and was the Jesse Root Professor of Law at the University of Connecticut School of Law, where he taught from 1998-2007.

He was a Visiting Global Scholar at the University of London, Queen Mary's College in 2016-18 and a Distinguished Scholar in Residence at the Centre for Transnational Studies at the University of Bremen, Germany in 2014. He also served two terms on the Organizing Committee of the Association for the Study of Law, Culture, and the Humanities and was Co-Chair of the International Law and Technology Interest Group of the American Society of International Law.

In 1988, Berman graduated summa cum laude from Princeton University and earned his law degree from New York University in 1995. During law school, he served as Managing Editor of the NYU Law Review and received the University Graduation Prize for the graduating law student with the highest cumulative grade point average. He later clerked for Chief Judge Harry T. Edwards of the United States Court of Appeals for the District of Columbia Circuit and for Justice Ruth Bader Ginsburg of the Supreme Court of the United States.

INTERVIEW

Q: Will you please introduce yourself?

A: My name is Paul Schiff Berman. I'm currently the Walter S. Cox Professor of Law at The George Washington University Law School in Washington, D.C. I've had a long and varied career path both before law school and after I entered law.

As a Princeton undergraduate, I never thought about going to law school. I'd been involved in theater as a high school student, working on professional shows in New York City. At Princeton, I continued to direct shows and I also led the student-run theater there. All I wanted to do was to form my own theater company and to direct shows in New York.

So, after graduating from Princeton in 1988, I went to New York City and formed my own theater company just as I had promised myself. I directed a number of shows over the next eight years. The shows were created through a group process by our entire team of directors, actors, musicians, writers, and so forth. Over six to eight months we'd build a script, rehearse it for another month or so, and then present it in New York City. That was what I most wanted to do with my life at the time, so that's what I did. Law wasn't part of the picture then.

Q: Did you have good business sense?

A: I directed shows for my own company, and we usually broke even and got some government grants and contributions and things like that. In addition, I took on a series of freelance arts administration jobs that would allow me to make a living while doing theater. I worked as administrative director for a more established theater company, did some bookkeeping for an arts funding foundation, and did administrative work for a dance company. When you combined all those activities, I was able to make enough money to live on.

Q: How did you get into law?

A: I have to say I'm not someone who does a huge amount of specific planning. There are people who think, "Well, here's where I want to be five or ten years from now. What steps do I have to take to get there?" That isn't the way I look at my life at all. I look at life more as an ongoing improvisation. Maybe it's related to the theater work I did earlier.

I've always believed you should do whatever it is that most excites, energizes, and activates you at the present moment. And then assume that if you do that thing, whatever it is, to your utmost and at the highest level possible, new doors will open and new opportunities will arise. Then, you have to be willing to jump at those opportunities. Do them to the best of your ability with as much energy, and focus, and passion, and drive as you have, and again something else will show up.

So, there came a point where I had formed the theater company and I was keeping it afloat financially. I saw how I could make a living as a theater director in New York City. I then started thinking, "Okay, I'm doing what I've always wanted to do with my life. Now do I want to keep doing it?"

I slowly grew a little dissatisfied with only doing theater. I wanted to be more involved in tangibly helping real people in the real world do things. Also, I wanted to be more directly engaged in social and political issues facing the country. So, I started thinking about how I might do that.

Over the next couple of years, I started thinking about law school. I was always vaguely interested in law. I'd done debating in junior high school and high school a little bit. And, I had majored in cultural anthropology as an undergraduate. What I liked about anthropology was that it was the study of the many ways in which different cultures and different groups within cultures construct meaning from reality. One of the exciting things about anthropology was to realize that the way you happen to look at the world isn't the only way to look at it and it isn't any more natural or inevitable than other ways of looking at it.

I thought of law as a similar exercise in thinking about the world from multiple points of view. One of the amazing things about lawyers is that they're the only people in society who are professionally committed to the idea that all points of view deserve to be heard, and also deserve to be articulated in as forceful and thoughtful way as possible. I thought that was pretty great, and I believe in that as an idea.

I never thought of my education as a path to a particular career. I saw education as something worth doing for the knowledge, the excitement, and for advancing greater understanding of the world.

And just as I went to college without a specific career in mind, I also went to law school without a specific path for law in mind. In fact, I went to NYU law school in large part because I wanted to stay in New York and continue directing shows. I wasn't sure I even wanted to be a lawyer. I just knew I was excited about law school. I gave myself a year off from theater, but then I got back into directing in my second and third years of law school, in part because I was still interested in theater, but also because I wasn't sure about the path I'd take in law. It was certainly plausible that I'd go back into theater after law school.

Q: During your transition from theater to law, how supportive were your family and friends?

A: My parents loved the fact that I did theater. They liked coming to my shows, and I would also tell them about other shows my friends and other people were putting on. They liked the idea of me exercising my creative talents. So, unlike many parents who yearn for their kids to take up a more "practical" career, I think my parents were actually a little disappointed initially when I said I might go into law, because they saw that as a little bit more staid and less creative. They were supportive, of course, but a little sad. Later they saw how energized I was by my life in law so I think that initial disappointment receded.

Interestingly, all my theater friends saw law as something very exciting and even cool! Conversely, the people I meet in law think my theater director career is cool. So I guess I get a benefit from having straddled both worlds.

Q: Did you think you could implement some sort of social change when you got into law?

A: Yes. I had a sense from popular culture that lawyers can help effectuate real change in the world. You think about the famous legal cases from history and even less well-known cases where real change happens at a large societal level because of law. And even just in an ordinary case, if a lawyer represents someone, it empowers the client and could change lives, too. I had a vague sense of all that when I was thinking about law school. I don't think I had a specific career path for law in mind, however. I just remember thinking law could be as exciting to me in the years to come as theater had been in the years I'd just spent. I wanted to continue to live a life that was full and energized.

When I went to law school, my initial thought was that I might want to be a criminal defense attorney, but ultimately I changed my mind about that after interning at a public defender's office. What public defenders do is crucial and I am in awe of their commitment, but in the end, for me, it just wasn't intellectually interesting enough.

Then I thought I'd become a civil rights attorney and form my own law practice, similar to the way I had started my own theater company. So, in the summer after my first year of law school, I interned for a private civil rights attorney in Cincinnati. I was fascinated to see how he had built a career on his own, doing only civil rights related work.

In my second year of law school, I also started getting interested in some of the theoretical sides of law. I took a wonderful course in the philosophy of law. I also took a course in legal history, and I started thinking of law as an academic pursuit. Some of my professors were encouraging me along those lines.

In the summer after my second year, people said I might want to try a big commercial law firm. So, I spent a summer in 1994 working for a firm in New York City representing commercial clients. That was also exciting and fun.

Ultimately, I applied for a post-graduate clerkship with a judge on the United States Court of Appeals for the District of Columbia circuit, and I clerked there for a year after law school.

Afterward, I was offered a position at the commercial law firm where I'd worked before, doing only prisoner civil rights cases for a year. It was called the "pro bono associate position." That seemed like a great combination of working with the resources of a big law firm but doing the kind of civil rights work I had done with the solo lawyer in Cincinnati.

Meanwhile, I also applied for another clerkship at the U.S. Supreme Court. In the following year, I was fortunate enough to get it.

Q: How did you get into teaching?

A: After clerking at the Supreme Court of the United States, obtaining a professor job became a more realistic possibility, and so I applied all around the country for teaching positions, not at all certain that I would get a job offer.

In 1998, I was hired as a law professor at the University of Connecticut Law School and I remained there through 2007. By that time, I had written numerous scholarly articles, gotten tenure, and written an Internet Law textbook that's used around the country. And I had started working on my first monograph, a full-length book that would bring together many of the ideas I had been developing in my articles.

But I remember I also started thinking, "Okay, what do I do now?" I was starting to feel a bit restless after nearly ten years as a law professor. And I believe that anytime you feel as if you're not fully engaged and excited, you need to think about what you can do to re-engage yourself.

And then, out of the blue, I got a call from Arizona State University (ASU), asking me if I might consider applying to be dean of its law school. This would be a significant shift for me, both because I had never been a university administrator and because I had never lived west of the Mississippi and didn't know anyone in Arizona. But the more I found out about the job opportunity at Arizona State, the more exciting it seemed. So, I took the leap and moved to Arizona, where I was dean for three years. I had an extraordinary time. We launched a whole range of new programs and initiatives, and the school went way up in the rankings of law schools. The quality of the student body increased, and our fundraising soared. It was an exciting and energizing experience.

Then I was offered the deanship at The George Washington University Law School. Although I loved being at ASU, I took the deanship at George Washington, mostly for family reasons. I was dean there for two years, and then the president and the provost of the university asked me to become their first vice provost for online education and academic innovation. This was at a time when online education was starting to become a major initiative for many universities. George Washington University needed some central strategic planning for online education, and having the opportunity to shape university-wide policy in this emerging educational area seemed very exciting.

I committed to three years as vice provost. When those three years came to an end in 2016, I went back to being a full-time professor. And after eight years as an administrator, being a full-time professor had become exciting for me again, so I dove back in to my scholarly life. In addition, I am now doing consulting work for two education-related start-up companies, and I'm even doing some appellate work representing clients.

That brings us to the present moment, and I don't know what's next in store for me. I just know that I'm always open to new opportunities.

Q: How important is passion in reaching your goals?

A: If you do something you're passionate about at a high level, I believe things will tend to work out. Now, it may be that for one reason or another, the thing you're most passionate about isn't providing enough income. That's okay; just build a life so that you can afford to do it. That may mean taking a second job. It may be finding some other sources of income. You can figure it out. But don't stop doing that thing you're passionate about.

It may turn out after a while that what you're doing on the side to make money actually becomes your passion. Or it may lead to yet a third thing. You don't know exactly. You just have to stay open to the possibilities that arise and go for what is most engaging. Too often, people decide on a plan and just single-mindedly pursue that plan. As a result, they aren't open to the possibility that serendipity might arrive and present new opportunities they didn't envision.

Q: How important is planning in reaching your goals?

A: The planned way of getting somewhere isn't necessarily the best way to get there. I'll give you an example. When I was in law school, I was on the student editorial board of the NYU Law Review. Most of the students on the board are more academically ambitious and a number of them were hoping to land a clerkship at the U.S. Supreme

Court. I remember some of these students planning and scheming and thinking of how to position themselves and their résumés to best appeal to a Supreme Court justice. One way they tried to do that was by writing articles for the law journal on constitutional theory, thinking it was the best way to impress a judge into hiring them as a clerk.

I, coming from theater and doing my own thing, was totally unwilling to play that whole game of trying to position myself for some future clerkship I might or might not get. Instead, influenced by my background in cultural anthropology, I wrote a law journal article on what would have to be the seemingly least practical topic one could write on: trials on animals and inanimate objects in Medieval Europe and Ancient Greece.

Fast forward a couple of years. When I was applying for a Supreme Court clerkship, I included that article as the writing sample with my application. And Justice Ginsburg happened to pick up my file and read my article the same week that the Supreme Court was hearing an argument in a case involving the contemporary legal doctrine of civil forfeiture, which actually derives from that old history of trials of inanimate objects and animals in Medieval Europe.

Justice Ginsburg saw the connection to her case and was intrigued by my article. I'm convinced to this day that the article was part of the reason I was hired as a clerk, whereas it turned out that most of the people who wrote on constitutional theory were not. That shows that you can't predict what's going to help you later in life and what's going to be the thing that opens the door. So I believe you might as well do what excites you and what you're interested in, and not worry about trying to be overly strategic. Just be who you are. Some door or doors will open somewhere sometime. You cannot predict it.

It seems to me that people spend a lot of time planning and trying to position themselves and not enough time jumping in and pursuing their passion.

Q: Why do you think our current education system doesn't leave us open to seizing opportunities and being willing to take risks?

A: A lot of human activity is governed by fear: fear of the future, fear of the unknown, and fear of failing. So, we try to do things to minimize risk. And it may be that the educational system is designed, in part, around minimizing risk. I hear all the time about students getting an education to "keep options open" or "create a marketable set of skills." I guess that's not a bad thing, but I want people to think of education as not just a means to an end, but as an intensely exciting and mind-expanding experience on its own.

With that being said, I can remember plenty of examples in my own life where I've encountered educators who haven't been risk averse, and who've been extraordinarily inspiring to me. So, certainly the opposite exists. But I fear it's not the dominant culture.

Q: What are your greatest successes or accomplishments so far?

A: I've always loved to create an environment where other people feel safe to have ideas and then I would work to help them take those ideas and fly.

When I was doing theater, we would do improvisations, and with any remotely interesting idea that arose, we would give it a try. And I found that the good ideas would snowball and lead to more ideas, while the less generative ideas would fall away.

As a professor, I always try to create a similar improvisational space in the classroom to activate students' creativity.

As a dean, I'd get ideas from faculty members, students, alumni, and practitioners about programs or initiatives the law school could engage in. My response, coming from theater, was, always, "Okay, let's try it." And if we didn't have the resources to fully implement the idea, I would see if I could at least launch a pilot version of the idea to see if I could get people excited about it. After all, money tends to follow excitement because people tend to invest once they see a good idea rolling forward. And if an idea ultimately didn't work or didn't generate sufficient excitement, that's okay; we would just stop pursuing that particular idea and try something different. The point is to create a culture of innovation and risk-taking.

I've always tried to create that sort of environment among those around me, where they'd be fulfilled to the greatest degree possible, they'd be energized to the greatest degree possible, and their talents would be utilized to the greatest degree possible. One of the great joys about working with students is that I can open conceptual or practical doors that might completely transform their career path or their way of thinking about law and their role in it. And then they go out in the world and work on important issues and change other peoples' lives through their legal work. It's an exciting cycle of continuous transformation.

Q: Do you think online education has value?

A: Yes. It's sometimes over-hyped, but it certainly has value and potential. As a world society, we've created extraordinary educational institutions that provide an amazing education, but only to a small slice of the world's population. It would be transformative to the world if more people had access to such top-level education.

The key is to provide multiple pathways, so people from different backgrounds and perspectives, with different kinds of life experiences and choices and financial circumstances, can discover some pathway that works for them to get access to this amazing education.

Online is one such pathway. Having now supervised more than a hundred online degree and certificate programs at George Washington University and having watched many others, I'm completely convinced that you can deliver incredibly high-quality education online that's every bit as good as what you'd find on campus, so long as the university puts the time, thought, and resources into making online education work well.

As a result, we now can provide access for a motivated student who for whatever reason cannot relocate to these universities to get a high quality education. That's really significant. Online education helps expand the opportunities.

Again, the key is that we have to create more pathways so that more differently situated students can find a way into the educational system, because broader access to education is essential to transform the world.

ACTION GUIDE

An easy reference guide to the advice and tips provided by Paul Berman

1) Keep An Open Mind

Having a plan for your life and career is fine, but keep a watchful eye for unexpected opportunities that may come your way and take you in a new direction.

2) Pursue Your Passion

You can't predict what's going to help you later in life, so you might as well do what excites you and not worry about it. Some door or doors will open for you somewhere.

3) Create An Environment Where New Ideas Are Welcome

I've always loved to create an environment where other people feel safe to have ideas and then I would work to help them take those ideas and fly. When I was doing theater, we would do improvisations, and with any remotely interesting idea that arose, we would give it a try. And I found that the good ideas would snowball and lead to more ideas, while the less generative ideas would fall away.

4) Don't Overlook Online Education Opportunities

Having supervised more than a hundred online degree and certificate programs and having watched many others, I'm completely convinced that you can experience incredibly high quality education online that's every bit as good as what you'd find on campus, so long as the university puts the time, thought, and resources into making online education work well.

CHAPTER 3

Sarah Buel

BIOGRAPHY

"The odds were stacked against me going to Harvard. At times, I acted out as a teen. I went to eight different high schools, I got into some trouble, and I started out in community colleges. I was a single parent and I was interested in domestic violence. I was told I didn't have a chance. Then the most amazing miracle happened. They let me in and gave me a full scholarship."

~ Sarah Buel

Sarah Buel, J.D., is a lawyer and anti-domestic violence activist, who retired in 2016 as a Clinical Professor of Law at the Sandra Day O'Connor College of Law at Arizona State University. Being a survivor of domestic violence herself, she became an impassioned advocate for battered women and abused children. She overcame adversity and followed her dream of being a Harvard Law School graduate in order to best defend and advocate.

Buel's path to becoming a lawyer was not a short or easy one. Despite not having a Bachelor's Degree, she got a job as a paralegal at New Hampshire Legal Aid. There she realized she must go to college and get a degree so she could go to law school and truly help those in need. In 1987, after seven long years of taking night classes, she earned her Bachelor of Arts from Harvard Extension School. She then graduated cum laude from Harvard Law School in 1990.

Buel was a Clinical Professor at The University of Texas School of Law where she started and co-directed the Domestic Violence Clinic. She also co-founded the National Center on Domestic and Sexual Violence. From 1995—97, she served as special counsel for the Texas District and County Attorneys Association after spending six years as a prosecutor in Massachusetts. In 2010, she was recruited by the Sandra Day O'Connor College of Law at Arizona State University, where she taught Domestic Violence and the Law, Evidence, Human Trafficking, and Professional Responsibility courses.

Buel has received numerous recognition and awards in the many years she has worked with abused women and children. In 1991, she received the Boston Bar Association's Public Service Award. In 1992, she received the Massachusetts Bar Association's Outstanding Young Lawyer's Award and the American Bar Association's Top Twenty Young Lawyer's Award. In 1992, she narrated the Academy-Award winning documentary, "Defending Our Lives." In 1996, she was named one of the five most inspiring women in America by NBC.

She also received the American College of Obstetricians and Gynecologists' Public Service Award in 1997, the University of Texas Law Fellowships Public Service Award in 1998, the National Organization of Victim Assistance Allied Professional Award in 1999, the American Bar Association's Fellows Award in 2001, and the Harvard Law School Gary Public Service Award in 2002, and the ASU Centennial Professor Award in 2013. In 2015, the ABA gave her its 20/20 Vision Award.

INTERVIEW

Q: Will you please introduce yourself?

A: My name is Sarah Buel, and I recently retired as Clinical Professor of Law at the Sandra Day O'Connor College of Law at Arizona State University in Tempe, Arizona.

I knew I wanted to be a lawyer when I was about 12. I had been frustrated watching my wonderful, sweet, kind, amazing mother, who was raising her five kids and her sister's two kids on and off. We were quite poor. But, she always had a positive attitude.

When I started babysitting at age 12, I got to "meet" Perry Mason on TV. That changed my life. He knew how to make the right things happen in the courtroom. So, I thought, "Okay, I want to be a lawyer. I want to be able to speak up for people like my mother, who aren't able to speak up for themselves."

I was also intrigued with the civil rights movement. I could only follow it on the radio and through an old Life magazine we got from a neighbor. I thought, "Wow, I want to be part of that, too. I want to figure out how to help people who are being mistreated – whether it's because they're poor or of color."

My parents got divorced when I was 12, and because I didn't want to choose between them, I left home and went to live with a family in New York. I ended up going to eight different high schools, for a lot of reasons. All of them were great learning experiences.

Q: Did you go to university immediately after high school?

A: No, I married my high school sweetheart. He had not been abusive while we were dating, although I didn't realize that his extremely controlling behavior could be a predecessor. I thought only people who drank were violent, because that's the only time I saw my father and his friends get crazy. I thought if I married someone who wasn't an alcoholic, he wouldn't be abusive.

But, then he turned out to be violent. I went to court and the judge told me, "Be more patient and don't do things that aggravate him."

I went to a family priest and he said, "Maybe you cook too much Italian food. Try diversifying the menu."

The greatest thing that happened was my son being born in 1975. But, the abuse continued. I had left a few times, but I kept going back because I wanted to save my marriage and I wanted my son to grow up with his father. Finally in the summer of 1977, I left my husband and didn't return.

Q: How did you get on track to becoming a lawyer?

A: There was a wonderful federal job training program (CETA) and through that I got a job as a paralegal with Legal Aid. That was a gift from heaven. I had a wonderful boss, Mark Larsen.

First, it was a miracle that I got hired, because the office was in New Hampshire and there were a number of applicants with degrees. I said, "I know I only have a high school diploma, but I'll fight harder than anybody else. And I'm so hungry to learn." So, they gave me that chance. It was amazing.

I got to do a lot. Through legal services, we started the first shelters in New Hampshire, we wrote the first abuse prevention laws, and we started coordinating with people in other states. I also started a

Women & Children (WIC) Nutritional Feeding Program for several rural counties through the Department of Agriculture.

Q: Why did you leave that job?

A: I realized I needed to go to college to earn a degree and go to law school. I needed a school that had scholarship funds available. I applied to Harvard, Yale and Columbia. I did some reading in the library and realized they were top-notch schools. Columbia let me in.

I moved back to New York and started at Columbia. I had fabulous professors for writing, public speaking, and English. Physics was another story – that about killed me – but I did have a great professor and got a B.

Q: Were people supportive or dismissive of your decision to become a lawyer?

A: From early on, I didn't have teachers supportive about college, and when I was in eighth grade, I was told I shouldn't think about college, and that I should go more for secretarial work. That enraged me so much. They looked at me and my family. My older sisters were having troubles, my father had issues because he walked out on us when I was nine, and it was the whole "wrong-side-of-the-tracks" stereotype.

When I started at Columbia, I remember my father saying something to me along the lines of, "Don't worry if you don't do well at Columbia. There are lots of other jobs. You can go back to being a paralegal or secretary." I remember seething; I was so enraged.

Q: How did you overcome your lack of support?

A: I credit my mother 100 percent. One of the gifts from her was that she kept telling me, "You can do anything you put your mind to." She also always had unconditional positive love for us – her children. She's the kindest person you'll ever meet, and she never thinks about what's in it for her. She does what she thinks is the right thing to do. Growing up, she helped lots of others in need, even when we had nothing.

Another part of it was my stubbornness. Also, it feels so good when you do the right thing and help people. I realized the only way I could do that was by getting this law degree.

Q: Why did you leave Columbia?

A: For several reasons relating to my safety, I realized I needed to get out of New York. So, I transferred to Stanford because they had this amazing program – The Stanford Workshop on Political and Social Activities. Because I had done well at Columbia, I got a scholarship to go there.

I sold everything I had in New York and drove across country to Stanford. When I got there, I was told, "You shouldn't have been given financial aid! Our policy is not to give financial aid to transfer students. So, you can come here, but with no financial aid."

Even back then, Stanford was expensive. They told me I'd get financial aid after a year but, as a single mother, I knew it wasn't going to work. So, I had moved all the way out there for nothing.

Q: Is that how you ended up at Harvard?

A: I remembered hearing that Harvard has an extension school in Cambridge. All the classes were held in the evening at Harvard.

I called them and they offered a grant to cover my tuition. So I moved all the way across the country again and started a job at Legal Services and started at the Harvard Extension School that fall. It was a gift from heaven.

Q: Did you finish your degree?

A: I was at Legal Services for a few years, until budget cuts eliminated the non-lawyer jobs. My youngest brother was going to school at the

University of Colorado, Boulder. So, I thought I'd go out to Denver. I also had a friend who had some contacts at Legal Aid in Denver. On my 30th birthday, I drove across country to Denver with my brother.

I went to Legal Aid and was told, "Oh no, we have the same budget cuts, so we can't hire anyone." But a lady at Legal Aid had a contact at a law firm in Denver and told me they were looking for a paralegal.

When I applied at the law firm, they were so impressed that I'd attended Harvard. I didn't even have my degree yet; I'd only gone to night school for two years. But, I did have some writing samples with me. They said, "Okay, one big problem is too many of our lawyers hate to write. If you can write, come on over."

That was fabulous. At Legal Aid, I was only making $11,000. But at that law firm I was going to make $15,000.

I put in long hours there. My way of dealing with stress and personal issues is to avoid them by doing more work. So, I got on different boards, including that of the local shelter in Denver and volunteered there. I also volunteered with a wonderful children rights clinic.

I had a great time my first year there, but I didn't go to school; I arrived too late to apply. I decided, "I'm not doing this again. I have to be in night school. I'm not going to be deterred from becoming a lawyer."

I was going to stay in Denver, but then a cousin who lived in Seattle said, "Washington has passed a mandatory arrest law, greatly increasing the prosecutors' caseloads. So, the Seattle City Attorney is hiring advocates – not lawyers. And they want people with legal services experience. You have to come and see! They're even paying $19,000."

So I scraped up the money to fly there with my son, and I had the interview. I was offered the job and I thought, "Okay, I have to do this." This was going to be the first time in my life I got to work one hundred percent in domestic violence.

I started at the Family Violence Project at the Seattle City Attorney's Office, and it was wonderful. I got to be an advocate, reading police reports in the morning, interviewing the victims, and then racing over to court for the trials. My approach was, "Whatever the survivor needs, we'll do it."

Q: Did you continue your education while you were in Seattle?

A: I started at the University of Washington at night, and had some great professors. One of them said to me, "You can stay here and graduate from the University of Washington and you'll be a big fish in a little pond. But, you have real potential and you need to go to a good school – some place that will give you a scholarship and the credentials you need to go to law school. You need that."

I thought if I went back to the Harvard Extension School I could at least be in the Boston area when I finished and I could have a chance to go to Harvard Law School. So, I moved back across country again.

Q: How did you support yourself when you returned to Harvard?

A: I was hired by Patrick Hamilton, the head of the Massachusetts Committee on Criminal Justice. After a surge in domestic violence, sexual assault, and child abuse murders in Massachusetts, the Governor wanted someone to coordinate policy and planning for the state, and I was given that task. Mr. Hamilton and I were part of starting the Governor's Domestic Violence Commission, through which we were able to remedy gaps in police and judicial training, and spur reforms to the Judicial Conduct Commission.

There were a number of high profile domestic violence cases that had been mishandled by police and courts. We had an ally at The Boston Globe, a reporter named Eileen McNamara, who won a Pulitzer Prize for writing about these issues – which kept them in the news. And she helped us use these tragedies to spur needed reforms.

Q: How did you get into Harvard Law School?

A: As I was nearing college graduation, I asked my boss to write a letter of recommendation for me. I told him I wanted to go to Harvard Law School because people would listen to me with that credential, plus they had the money to give me a scholarship.

He said, "I don't think you understand. You aren't really the type Harvard looks at."

The odds were stacked against me. At times I acted out as a teen. I went to eight different high schools, was sometimes in trouble, and started at community colleges. I was a single parent interested in domestic violence. I was told I didn't have a chance.

The most amazing miracle happened. I was not only admitted, but I got a full scholarship.

One of my recommendation letters said I "revolutionized poverty law in New Hampshire and dragged us all kicking and screaming into the notion of holistic services and got us to look at other poverty issues." And the letter from my boss, Patrick Hamilton, talked about all the legislative, judicial, police, and policy reforms we accomplished in Massachusetts.

Eileen McNamara wrote an unsolicited letter for me as well. She said, "I never would have gotten the Pulitzer Prize without Sarah Buel. Nobody else would talk to me, and she would let me use her name. You have to let her in." I'm sure that didn't hurt either.

In the fall of 1987, I started law school and was so happy to be there, I wanted to kiss the floor every morning.

Q: Did you launch any programs while you were at Harvard Law School?

A: I co-founded the Battered Women Advocacy Project with fellow law student Suzy Groisser. I put an ad in the student newspaper, and 78 students showed up for the first meeting. By the end of the year, we had 130 students providing court advocacy with victims, legal research, and fundraising for local shelters. It's still one of the largest organizations – but they've changed the name to be gender neutral.

Then I started a Women in Prison project. There were outrageous things going on in women's prisons, in part because the female inmates were too afraid to speak up.

During summer between my first and second year, I got a grant from Harvard to work at the women's prison under the auspices of the Massachusetts Coalition of Battered Women Service Groups. As I taught the battered women in prison about their legal rights, researched their cases, and advocated for them to have visitation with their children, I learned their stories.

Then I started working with Stacey Kabat on a documentary film called Defending Our Lives, which won an Academy Award in 1994.

When I went back for my second and third year, I was in the Legal Aid Bureau for 20 hours per week. I wasn't sure if I wanted to go to legal aid or a prosecutor's office from law school. I was also interested in juvenile defense.

Q: What did you do after graduating from law school?

A: I started in a prosecutor's office, but had an abusive boss. So, one of my good friends in the Norfolk County DA's office recommended that I interview to start the first Domestic Violence Unit in a DA's office in Massachusetts.

There I was eight months out of law school and was hired. Bill Delahunt, the Norfolk County DA, hired passionate people and let us run with innovative projects as long as we could offer good reasons. We started a number of fabulous projects centered on a coordinated community response, because he was so supportive and genuinely cared about survivors and all in need.

After my boss was elected to Congress, I decided to go to Texas. I had done some work for their Prosecutor's Association, and I mentioned my interest to the man in charge of training. He said, "We want to hire you as we need someone who'll go all over Texas and will help prosecutors with domestic violence cases and training. You'll certainly get to know the state."

I thought that was a great opportunity. And since my son had gone off to college, I went to Texas. I had a great time working for the Prosecutor's Association, and I did get to know Texas by driving everywhere.

Q: How did you begin teaching about domestic violence?

A: While I was in Boston, some Boston College law students said to me, "We need a course on domestic violence, because we want to be corporate attorneys and prosecutors. We need to learn the things you're talking about for our job placements and internships." They approached their dean and said they wanted me to teach this course.

The dean asked me to put together a syllabus for the course. I was told, "If you don't get four students, you can't teach." I ended up with 60 students my first year. I had a great time, and I learned a lot about teaching.

Q: Did you teach at any other universities?

A: I went to the University of Texas and said I wanted to teach this same course as an adjunct professor. I was told: "Look, unless you went to Harvard and you've done some writing, we're not interested."

"Well, actually I did go to Harvard and I've done a fair amount of writing," I said.

"Oh," he said, "Well, maybe we can talk."

So I taught Domestic Violence and the Law for 14 years. In 2000, a new dean asked if I'd like to teach a torts course, too. I also co-taught the clinic course and went on to teach criminal law and an education seminar.

Q: How did you end up at Arizona State University?

A: I was happy in Texas, but then the dean at Arizona State University recruited me to come because he had secured funding for a center for family justice. It was with the promise that I could expand my work into trafficking and human rights – which I had wanted to do.

So in 2010, I came to ASU. I loved the students and my supportive colleagues there. I also enjoyed community work, such as serving as president of the board for the National Advocacy and Training Network and their SEEDS transitional shelters for high risk abuse survivors.

Q: How important was passion in pursuing your goal?

A: Oh, absolutely, I've always been passionate about this work and about social justice. One of my greatest hopes was to inspire my students to be champions for social justice – whether writing big checks or volunteering, or making it their life work.

Q: What's been your greatest success or accomplishment?

A: There are a few, but by far the most important is my son, Jacey. He has always been my greatest joy and I continue to learn more from him than anyone – he teaches that there are two things a person can control: how hard you try and how you treat others. He is Entrepreneurship Education Director for The Possible Project, teaching indigent youth how to start and run their own businesses while finishing high school and going to college.

Second, it was helping to start the battered women's shelters in New Hampshire and write those first laws. That was tremendously empowering to learn I could advocate, that I had a gift for talking, for being able to persuade people, and for learning early on the reasons to do that.

The third was starting a Supplemental Nutrition Programs for Women, Infants and Children (WIC) and three summer lunch programs in New Hampshire. Those were for destitute communities. It was heartbreaking when kids told me that when they weren't getting free breakfast and lunch in school, and that sometimes all they had to eat all day was a candy bar. Providing them with some sustenance was very rewarding.

My fourth was narrating the Defending Our Lives documentary, and helping the women who had only fought back in self-defense get out of prison, and instituting some reforms there.

Fifth was helping to change the judicial conduct guidelines in Massachusetts. I'm grateful for the courage to speak up to The Boston Globe and allowing the paper to use my name, because otherwise the story of judicial misbehavior didn't have much credibility. Through our domestic violence roundtables, we started court watch programs that documented state misconduct on many levels and resulted in key reforms.

Finally, I'm very proud of co-founding the Domestic Violence Clinic with Jeana Lungwitz at the University of Texas, which flourished under her direction.

ACTION GUIDE

An easy reference guide to the advice and tips provided by Sarah Buel

1) You Do Not Have Because You Do Not Ask

This proverb is true in a broad sense, and especially in relation to networking. Many times, others will go out of their way to help you if they know you're aspiring for something great. One of my recommendation letters said I "revolutionized poverty law in New Hampshire and dragged us all kicking and screaming into the notion of holistic services and got us to look at other poverty issues." And the letter from my boss, Patrick Hamilton, talked about all the legislative, judicial, police, and policy reforms we accomplished in Massachusetts.

2) Believe in Yourself When No One Believes in You

Loved ones, teachers, even bosses are capable of encouraging you to "set the bar low." They may be well meaning, dealing with their own insecurities, or even malicious in their advice, but don't let them decide your future.

As I was nearing college graduation, I asked my boss to write a letter of recommendation for me. I told him I wanted to go to Harvard Law School. He said, "I don't think you understand. You aren't really the type Harvard looks at." The odds were stacked against me. I was told

I didn't have a chance. The most amazing miracle happened. I was not only admitted, but I got a full scholarship.

3) Be an Integral Piece in the Puzzle, and Allow Others to Do the Same

Whether or not you're able to own your project for its entire life cycle, don't let your desire to micromanage stand in the way of its progress. Allow others to play an integral part in carrying out their passions too.

4) When You Don't Have Experience, Ambition Helps

There was a wonderful federal job training program (CETA) and through that I got a job as a paralegal with Legal Aid…First, it was a miracle that I got hired, because the office was in New Hampshire and there were a number of applicants with degrees. I said, "I know I only have a high school diploma, but I'll fight harder than anybody else. And I'm so hungry to learn." So, they gave me that chance. It was amazing.

5) If You Think Something Should Change, Be the Change Agent

No matter your age, young or old, rich or poor, experienced or inexperienced, find out what the small steps are to making a change, and get the ball rolling. I co-founded the Battered Women Advocacy Project with fellow law student Suzy Groisser. I put an ad in the student newspaper, and 78 students showed up for the first meeting. By the end of the year, we had 130 students providing court advocacy with victims, legal research, and fundraising for local shelters.

CHAPTER 4

David Medina

BIOGRAPHY

"I always like to recommend that people invest in themselves. At the end of the day, you can't take away my law degree and my experience. No matter how difficult things can get, you can't take away who I am."

~ David Medina

David Medina is a recent graduate of the Sandra Day O'Connor College of Law at Arizona State University, served as a clerk for the Honorable Nora Barry Fischer at the U.S. District Court in the Western District of Pennsylvania, and is currently an intellectual property lawyer with Orrick, Herrington & Sutcliffe.

He wasn't always interested in law. During his secondary school years, at El Rancho High School in Pico Rivera, California, his academic interests were in mathematics and economics.

Following high school graduation, Medina attended Stanford University, where he pursued a degree in Management Science and

Engineering, with a focus on finance. At the same time, he founded Flashworks Inc., a company to help teachers better manage their paperwork through digitizing documents. After graduating, he worked as a product manager for a startup that built infrastructure to allow people to cheaply and safely send money from the U.S. to Mexico.

In 2012, Medina started working toward earning a law degree. His focus was on intellectual property – a field where he could combine his legal education with his engineering background. He did very well in law school, receiving the Willard H. Pedrick Scholar award almost every semester (ASU's version of the honor roll), the Gold 'N Gavel Scholar award, and graduating magna cum laude. During his time as a law student, David also interned for the U.S. Court of Appeals for the Federal Circuit, worked as a Spring Writing Intern for a well-respected Phoenix law firm, and clerked for the firm he would later join full-time.

INTERVIEW

Q: Will you please introduce yourself?

A: My name is David Medina, and I'm a recent graduate of the Sandra Day O'Connor College of Law, and a former federal district court law clerk. I currently practice law as an IP litigator in California.

The best place for me to start would be with my family. One conversation jumps out to me in particular. When my siblings and I (I'm the oldest of three) were little, my dad proclaimed that my sister would be a teacher, my brother would be a lawyer, and I would be an engineer. As things turned out, my dad wasn't too far off. My sister just graduated with an education degree and is pursuing her credentials to become a teacher. My brother and I flip-flopped paths; he's a software engineer, and I'm the one who ended up graduating from law school. Go figure.

I grew up in Southern California in the relatively small town of Pico Rivera. It's one of those cities where, if you don't have anything to compare it to as a child, you think it's pretty much perfect. The community is supportive, and everyone's out there helping one another. People are generally friendly. It's not until you start comparing it to other cities that you realize some of the differences that arise from growing up in that area and that environment.

In my high school, roughly 98 percent of students were Mexican-American. We were all pretty much the same. Some of the richest kids were middle class and some of the poorest were about as poor as you can be. Our school was built to house 750 kids, but when I was there we had about 4,000.

Up through high school, I fancied myself as an engineer, as a mathlete, and as a science guy. In middle school, I competed in a mathematics competition and, in high school, I joined the Academic Decathlon, a competition that tested students on ten different academic subjects. Although everyone on the team had to study every subject, people naturally specialized in one field or another. I decided early on to become an expert in the subjects others were afraid of or didn't like.

I decided to become the best at the tough subjects for two reasons. First, I strongly believed that anyone can learn anything if given enough time. Second, I concluded that I could best help the team if I could master those subjects. From as far back as I could remember, I've been comfortable explaining things, especially complex topics, to my friends. And so, I tackled the hardest subjects in an effort to make them more understandable to those around me. In the Academic Decathlon, the toughest subject for us was economics, so I made a goal to be the best in it. Like any new area of study, economics had a certain amount of jargon I had to master to be able to understand what was going on. So, after putting in the time to learn the jargon, I became the economics whiz on the team.

Reflecting on how things turned out, it was remarkable that we performed as well as we did. With nothing more than the support of a few teachers and essentially our own willpower, we would perennially rank in the top end of the entire region, despite not having any of the resources other schools in the region had.

But, our success in the Academic Decathlon was not the norm. At my high school, the vast majority of students didn't go to college. There were 730 students in my senior class, and I don't believe more than 40 or 50 went on to a four-year university right out of high school. The majority who were interested in pursuing higher education ended up going to community college. Even that number was pretty sparse. It was sad, but the vast majority believed they had only three options: work at some labor-intensive job, go to jail, or join the military. Nobody said or enforced that belief, but it felt like those were the realities of what you could do outside of school.

Luckily for me, I stayed motivated and focused throughout school. I was the third-ranked kid in my class, and ended up going to Stanford. I was confident coming out of high school that I could take on pretty much anybody. In high school, I thought I could do anything. I played football, I played varsity tennis, and I played four different musical instruments. I was good in math, I took all the AP classes available, and I even took classes at the local community college. In my mind I could do no wrong. But when I arrived at Stanford, it was an entirely different ballgame. Stanford exposed just how little I knew.

Q: How did you decide on your major?

A: Despite my initial cockiness, I didn't even know what to pick for my major. When you first get there, they give you a book with all of the degrees listed, and let you pick. You can go in and talk to people if you need help, but as a young, stubborn 18-year-old, I was pretty confident I'd be able to figure it out. I ended up just going to my roommate, who had a totally different background and different life goals, and asking him what he thought was a good major.

He said, "Management, science, and engineering."

I said, "Great. Sign me up." That was it. There was no more thinking on that route. In hindsight, that was a horrible way of doing things, but luckily, I ended up making the most of that decision.

Q: How did you cope with the academic stress?

A: Everyone has stuff they struggle with, but in my opinion, you can separate resilient people from others by their ability to cope with the stress in a way that allows them to succeed. Although not ideal, I coped with my stress by shifting my energy into extra-curricular activities.

I was so enthralled with the idea of doing anything outside of campus that I co-founded the racquetball club, I started a company, and I also did an abroad program in Japan – anything around me to escape the confines of the school.

In hindsight, I should have doubled down on my efforts to succeed academically, though I partially blame not doing so on my inexperience. A lot of why I made the decisions I did had to do with my background. For the first time in my academic career, I didn't know how to respond to adversity. To make matters tougher, my immediate family also lacked experience in how to handle the high demands of a premier university. My parents supported me with what they had, and they generally assumed everything would be hunky-dory. But it was tough learning how to succeed in that new environment.

Q: Were your parents your mentors?

A: My mom teaches first grade and my dad was a bus driver. So, my parents had limited exposure or understanding of other career paths. My uncles are mostly firefighters or cops, and the majority of their wives stay at home. So, nobody in my family had any clue how to pursue other career paths. We knew being a lawyer sounded nice, doctor sounded nice, and engineering sounded nice, but we knew little beyond that.

There wasn't much in the way of people being able to guide me through my career options. I don't know of any of my friends who had a parent who was an engineer, lawyer, doctor, or anyone with a professional degree. The parents I knew worked in factories or at other physical jobs.

My mother was the most educated person I knew, because she was a teacher. Teachers generally had the highest education of those I interacted with.

At Stanford, when my friends struggled in class, they'd go and talk to their dads, who were economists, or their moms, who were engineers. There was so much positive reinforcement from their parents who had attended Stanford, Yale, or Harvard. They were able to rely on them and get them through the tough times. The academic benefit from that type of network is invaluable but, unfortunately, I didn't have the same network available to me.

Based on my experiences, I'm convinced that mentorship isn't just nice, it's necessary. It's necessary particularly for those who don't have the background, the experience, or people they can lean on to help them understand what the next steps are. It's even more necessary for the people who have broken through the ceilings in their group. This is true because if you're the highest in your group, how do you get higher? I found that you can grow by learning from trial and error, or by having someone else with more experience show you the way. Because I didn't have a mentor at Stanford, I had to learn by trial and error.

Q: Did you do well at Stanford?

A: I made it through by keeping my head above water. It wasn't pretty. I now believe that I was not limited by intelligence. Success there had everything to do with understanding how the game was played, understanding the importance of how to rely on the resources available, and understanding how to do high quality work in a high pressure atmosphere while smiling.

Although I graduated (read: survived), I believe I screwed up at Stanford. I had the lowest GPA of anybody in my graduating class applying to law school. I was on academic probation my last year, and it took me five years to graduate, instead of four. I played the game about as wrong as anybody could play it. It wasn't until after graduating and deciding to go to law school that I started to piece all those struggles and failures and frustrations together to turn them into forcing me to think, "Okay, how am I going to do this right?"

That's where "Phase Two" for me began. Transitioning back from where I was academically to develop the mindset I'd need to survive in law school was where I first encountered self-leadership.

Q: What made you decide to go to law school?

A: As I mentioned, I felt I barely scraped through Stanford. I had poor job prospects and, to top it off, I graduated in 2009, which was a bad time for everyone. So, I went looking for work and did little things here and there. It wasn't until about two years after graduating that I really decided to put everything on pause and take a good hard look at the path before me.

Coming out of college, my plan was to become an investment banker or a consultant. After that didn't pan out, I figured I'd go get another degree, but I wasn't quite sure what way I wanted to go. I was looking at medical school (though I hate blood and guts) and law school or even getting a Ph.D. in Engineering.

While I was mulling over what type of degree to pursue, I came across an article in The Wall Street Journal about some legal issues involving Apple and Samsung. It was about someone claiming the other one owed them a billion dollars, and about all the iPhones that might not be allowed in the country. I really didn't understand what was going on, but when I read that article, I knew it sounded awesome. That tipped the scale, and I then decided I'd go to law school. I had no idea what those guys were doing with all the lawsuits, but anything that was powerful enough to bring two billion-dollar behemoths to the table was exciting enough for me to pursue. My decision was that simple.

I had no family, friends, or even parents of friends who were lawyers. I had only talked to a single lawyer once, when I was seeking to patent an idea I had when I started a company. I had zero experience with the ways of lawyers. It was pretty much happenstance the way it played out.

Q: What made you decide to go to ASU?

A: I originally was going to go to the University of San Francisco, but a few days before law school was about to start, the former dean of students at ASU called me and made me an offer I couldn't refuse. As part of it, ASU was willing to let me join the Center for Law, Science and Innovation, offered financial support, and told me they would strongly support me in everything I pursued. Despite the fantastic offer, I initially declined. I was just too comfortable with my current arrangements and didn't want to rock the boat. Luckily, the dean called me again and talked me through the amazing opportunity that had landed on my doorstep, and this time I was smart enough to accept it.

With one week until school started, I packed up my room and my car, drove from San Francisco to Phoenix, and started looking for an apartment with immediate availability. As soon as I found one, I moved in. That's how my law school career started.

Q: What sparked your interest in intellectual property?

A: When I showed up as a first-year student, I took a look at my options and what people were trying to sell me on in law school. Almost immediately, I found intellectual property. When I looked into it a little bit more, I found that, for one aspect of it, patent law, it really helped if you had an engineering background. The moment I found that out, I decided to pick that specialty because I'm a firm believer in taking advantage of opportunities that are uniquely available to you. I wanted to do something other students couldn't.

Q: Did you do well academically in law school?

A: I crushed law school. After feeling bad about my undergraduate performance, I was determined to commit as much time and energy as I needed to excel. And that's exactly what I did.

This time around, I made sure to take advantage of every opportunity available to me. After the first semester at ASU, professors explained what a clerkship was. Once I heard about it, I knew for me as a person, as a lawyer, and as a professional that I wanted and needed that experience.

So, I set out to do the best I could in everything I could to prepare me to get that shot. I made sure I was academically successful.

I took advantage of every opportunity and internship that became available, because I knew those were going to be the things that separated me from my peers, the things that stood with me, and the things that established the foundation of who I was going to be as a professional. Experiencing success in all the little things helped propel me to reach for and accomplish bigger things. It was a cycle that further added to my motivation to succeed, and things spiraled up from there.

After reflecting on my success in law school, I realize now that a lot of it had to do with focus. In middle school and high school, I did my homework, I read and I put in the time to succeed. During my undergraduate years, I didn't focus. I did everything else – I wanted to talk to people, I wanted to play video games, I wanted to go out, and do everything but study. So when I came back to law school, I said, "This is going to be where I crystallize who I am. I'm going to do it the way I did it when I was in high school, and get back to the basics." By putting in the time and focusing on my education, I succeeded in law school.

Q: What's been your greatest success or accomplishment?

A: I made it known early on in law school that I wanted to clerk for a judge. At the end of my first year, the dean told me she had a connection with a judge in Washington, D.C. who would be willing to look at my application.

I went through the interview process, and the next fall I was sitting there in D.C. I didn't realize the Federal Circuit building was about a hundred feet from the White House. It was right there! So that was quite possibly the greatest experience I'd had so far, showing up to work every day and saying, "Yep, that's the White House." That was one of my true wild moments of law school, and it inspired me to keep pushing and see how far I could go.

I also had an internship with the firm of Bowman and Brooke. I found it pretty interesting because that firm did product liability litigation for large auto manufacturers, particularly Japanese companies. Well, I'm a car guy. As a senior in college, I taught myself how to rebuild engines. So, I had all sorts of car interests, and I was on "Cloud Nine" working for them. On top of that, I studied Japanese while I lived in Japan during an internship, so the match between what Bowman and Brooke worked on and my personal interests couldn't have been better. Both those experiences were among my greatest during law school.

Q: What was your greatest miscalculation or failure?

A: In high school, I had swagger. I could do no wrong. In college, I lost my mojo. I could do no right. It was almost amazing how much I screwed up. Doing so poorly academically was my greatest failure.

The law school experience for me was how I got the swagger back. It was a return to form. I decided I was going back to the basics and do whatever I needed to do to succeed. I decided to flip the switch.

Q: What do you mean by 'flipping the switch?'

A: Flipping the switch means deciding you're going to change and giving it everything you've got. It doesn't guarantee that everything will be great, and that success will come easily. In fact, it's almost a guarantee of the opposite – that you're going to work harder, miss out on the fun parties, and avoid the fun things everyone around you is doing in order to succeed.

In a sense, flipping the switch is like making a promise to yourself that you'll be resilient, determined, and ready to commit everything you've got to your success and future. Flipping the switch means you're going to take ownership and be the one to say, "You know what? My future begins with me."

ACTION GUIDE

An easy reference guide to the advice and tips provided by David Medina

Broadly speaking, I always like to recommend that people invest in themselves. At the end of the day, even if you were to somehow cheat me out of all my possessions, you couldn't take away my law degree and my experience. No matter how bad things can get, you can't take away who I am.

As for some specific advice, here are five things I've learned in getting where I am:

1) Stop the Planning Phase and Do It

Reflecting on my life, things stagnated when I couldn't decide whether I was going to go into law, medicine, get a Ph.D., or whatever. But things changed when I decided to be a lawyer and pursued that goal with everything I had. You just have to do it. There's no substitute for performance.

2) Harness Your Intellectual Curiosity

If you can get to the point where everything interests you in at least some way, you won't put up the mental roadblocks that could hinder your ability to learn, and you won't put on blinders that prevent you from seeing opportunities that are out there.

3) Develop Strong Communication Skills

Continually work on your emotional intelligence by learning how to listen and interact better. You'll have to interact with people throughout your entire life, and it's easy to trample on feelings and make social mistakes. Those mistakes can hold you back. If you're good at interacting with people and making connections, others will be more responsive to your requests.

4) Learn to Tell a Story

If you can become a good storyteller, people will be more willing to listen to you.

5) Finally, Learn How to Reach Out to Others

Make everyone aware of what you're striving to accomplish in a way that doesn't rub them the wrong way. People love to help others out, but they can't help if they don't know what you're striving for. I made sure I told everyone I wanted to clerk after graduation, and it's a huge reason why I was able to do so.

CHAPTER 5

Thomas Nathan

BIOGRAPHY

"Passion is the key to life. If you're passionate about your family, our hobbies, and your work, you're truly a blessed person, because you're filled with potentially enjoyable moments wherever you go in your life."

~ Tom Nathan

Thomas J. Nathan is the senior partner of the Chicago-based Munday & Nathan law firm. He has tried numerous cases throughout more than 37 years of practice and has obtained multiple significant verdicts and settlements. While specializing in medical negligence and product liability litigation in Illinois, he has litigated complex cases in many states throughout the country.

Over the years, Nathan has handled many "front page" cases involving electrocution, road design defects, vehicular rollovers, police pursuits, and other cases of national interest. In addition to an active trial and litigation practice, he has taught trial advocacy and litigation strategy, and has authored articles on civil litigation. He has been recognized by the Trustees of the John Marshall Law School with The Spirit of John Marshall Award, and has repeatedly been selected for recognition by Leading Lawyers, Super Lawyers and Top Attorneys in Illinois, as published in Chicago Magazine.

Nathan graduated with a B.A: in History from Lawrence University, an M.A. in History from Northwestern University, and a J.D. from The John Marshall Law School. He is a member of the Society of Trial Lawyers, the American Association for Justice, the Illinois Trial Lawyers Association, the Chicago Bar Association, the Illinois State Bar Association, the American Bar Association and is a Fellow of the American Bar Foundation. He has served on boards of various institutions, including Ann & Robert H. Lurie's Children's Hospital, Francis W. Parker School, and Wilmette School District 39, as well as several local foundations.

INTERVIEW

Q: Will you please introduce yourself?

A: My name is Tom Nathan, and I'm an attorney practicing personal injury law in Chicago, specializing in catastrophic injury and medical malpractice. I've been doing this for 37 years in the Chicago area and around the country.

I grew up in Chicago and had the benefit of having two parents who were supportive, no matter what my brothers and I did. My mother was a consummate volunteer. In politics, she was always working at precinct levels, and always for the Democrat candidate. She also was a volunteer at multiple charities. Both my parents, particularly my mother, instilled a sense of social responsibility in me and the belief that I have an obligation every day of my life to give back to society and to make my community better, no matter where I live.

As my life progressed from grade school to high school, I volunteered and served on student government and things like that. When the Vietnam War happened, I was in college, and that heightened my sense of social responsibility and my commitment to social justice.

I left Lawrence University and started teaching at the Francis Parker School, a progressive school in Chicago. It was consistent with the philosophy of giving back and also educating younger people to have that sense of commitment – which was a cornerstone of the philosophy of the school.

During that time, I started graduate school at Northwestern with the intent of getting a Ph.D. in American history, and then teaching for the rest of my life. I focused on becoming more aggressive, in terms of how I participated.

A law degree, which I had always put in the back of my mind, made a lot of sense. So, I continued teaching through graduate school while in law school, and graduated from law school in 1978.

Q: Why did you specialize in injury and malpractice law?

A: I wasn't sure what area of law to get into when I graduated, which was fairly common for most young lawyers. I spent the first two years learning the greatest lessons of my life. Number one is that law is a brutal experience. I was hoping to accomplish things on a social level but something wasn't clicking. I was working with these two wonderful people who were committed to their clients every single day and were gratified in the work they were doing, but there was something missing for me. So, I left that firm and went to another one. But I had a similar dissatisfaction; the work I was doing wasn't meshing with my core being.

By sheer luck, I became friendly with a family that had a nice personal injury firm, and I joined them in 1981. There I had a realization that stayed with me through the years. Whatever we do in our profession, if it doesn't match our passion, it doesn't work. It's a reality. I found in law a home for my passion for social justice and passion for helping people who were the victims of human errors.

I started focusing in these specialty areas: malpractice and catastrophic injuries. It has taken me all over the country. From that time in the early 1980s, I've found great satisfaction every day in the work I perform, the purpose of that work, and the people it benefits (whether it's my client or the community in general).

That brought me to starting my own firm, Munday & Nathan, in 1991. It was basically a continuation of the ethics of the first firm I'd worked for, but a smaller version of it.

Q: How would you describe a typical day in your life?

A: I can't. My life is different every day. Some of the activities, such as interviewing clients or doing depositions, are the same, but every client is different and every case is different. Every day is a challenge because I'm learning something new, whether it's how to put up an electrical line on a power pole, or whether it's figuring out why someone cancelled a diagnosis. Every day is different and every day requires researching or listening to new areas of life, medicine, engineering, automotive, or whatever it may be; that I find intellectually challenging.

At the end of the day, when I'm in relaxing with some friends, I have so many stories to tell. Some are with twists and turns you'd never imagine, but always those cases are driven with the same goal: to have the greatest result for the clients, for the social good, and for the causes of client injuries.

Q: Is your career satisfying?

A: Absolutely. My partners look at me and ask when I'll quit, and I respond with the answer, "You'll probably retire before I do." It's been a delight and I look forward to more years of it being delightful.

Q: Is passion important?

A: When I started out in school, a bunch of my friends became lawyers, and a lot of them knew that was all they were ever going to do. I'm happy to say that most of them have meshed their passions with their specialty within the law. So, it was fun to grow up with people who have lived that principle of matching your career with your passion.

Passion is the key to life. If you're passionate about your family, your hobbies, and your work, you're truly a blessed person, because you're filled with potentially enjoyable moments wherever you go in your life. Then work becomes easier. It's certainly fun to see young lawyers coming through who are engaged enough with their souls and their minds with the work they do. They have the perspective to see that the battle they're fighting isn't a personal battle with them and their opposing counsel, but it's a battle for obtaining the truth, correcting something that's wrong, and getting remuneration for their clients in the process.

You can't educate anybody on these most human elements of what it takes to be an excellent lawyer. Everyone can go to law school and can come out with a degree and a knowledge base, but what you do with that is what makes you happy. The talent you have inside of you will come through and you'll be engaged in your days more or less depending on that component of passion. The more you're engaged with your passion, your effectiveness and your willingness to pay attention to detail will be enhanced dramatically.

Q: Did you have any mentors?

A: I was lucky in that I had two good mentors growing up as a lawyer. The first one was Harry Rosenberg, one of the finest men I've ever known. He specialized in trust and estates, and real estate. Though that wasn't my cup of tea, Harry realized that earlier and tried to bring in litigation to allow me to practice in that area.

I did my first deposition in an architecture and engineering case. Growing up, I'd never even held a hammer in my hand. This case involved malpractice against an architect, a roofer, and a builder. My office used to overlook a plaza, where circuses were staged from time to time. On this one August day when I was defending these three people, I was hearing a deposition from one of them. The man looked out the window and, seeing the circus, said, "Mr. Nathan, this is the most amazing day of my life."

I said, "Why's that?"

He responded with, "I've never been at two circuses at once."

From that point on, even though I'd been humiliated, I was always smart enough to know I didn't know everything and to admit when I didn't. But, Harry brought that case in so I could get some exposure.

Fred Lane was equally as profound a mentor to me. He taught me how to aggressively litigate and to never give up until everyone on the other side liked me at the end of the day. Also, he taught me how to be diligent in paying attention to the details and listening and to be a good trial lawyer.

Over the years, I've tried to pass along the legacy I received from these two men to the young lawyers who work with and for me and also to the law students to whom I speak.

Q: Did you have a lot of support when you decided to become a lawyer?

A: I had a good support group. A family member had gotten into some legal trouble, and I saw the devastation it had on him. It was a catalyst.

Also, when I was working on my history degree, there were no jobs. I was making $6,000 a year teaching high school. It seemed time to switch. Everyone was supportive. Whatever I did, my parents couldn't have been more supportive. They always said, "If this is what you want to do, then we're there with you."

I clearly had significant learning disabilities growing up. That was before they even knew there were learning disabilities – they thought something was wrong. But because of the support at home, I was set up to succeed. My parents never said, "You need to get A's or B's." They said, "Just do your best."

Q: How important is having a sense of self-direction?

A: Self-direction is important. I've been able to try things some people might walk away from. I fully believe in myself. Sometimes, I'll stay with a case longer than others might, and in the process may get a good result. At least, the belief I can do it keeps me doing it. It's not a blind belief, but it's worked more often than it hasn't.

Q: How do you deal with toxic and negative people?

A: In nearly every household or family or business, you may find one or more of those kinds of people. The hardest thing to do is to recognize negativity, toxicity, or anger, and disengage from it or not accept it when you encounter it.

Certainly in law, there are many angry people practicing it. It took me a long time to recognize that, in principle, I shouldn't allow myself to engage in the anger, or accept the anger of another person. I'll say to them, "I won't accept your anger. If you want to talk like that go talk to someone else. If you don't like my position, I'm not getting involved in this." Such behavior will blacken your day. It will blacken your night and you won't sleep. It truly is something to avoid.

Most times, people don't know how to disengage and get caught up in the anger or sorrow. It then becomes the innocent or non-angry person's life as well. It's good fortune to know when to step away.

Looking back at my life, I've certainly had that conflict. It's probably only been in the past ten years that I've been able to recognize the event, the dynamics of it, and the freedom to say, "Not my problem. I'm not going to let you make it my problem."

Sometimes, people who are important to you are genuinely unhappy and you engage in that with them, but that's different from toxicity.

Q: What's been your greatest success or accomplishment to date?

A: I wouldn't point to an event or a verdict. I'd point to a happy career.

Q: What's been your greatest failure or miscalculation?

A: Some might say I'm not a good businessman and don't know how to say "no," or put my foot down and do things my way. That has been a career-long personality defect for me.

Second, looking back, I should have bought an office building instead of paying millions of dollars in rent.

Q: Is it okay to fail?

A: I've certainly lost a lot of cases. I've won more than I've lost, but I don't consider losing a failure – it's only a loss. If I look back on the last 37 years I may not have been good as a lawyer in the first couple years of it. But I don't think anyone was harmed from my lack of passion, because I tried my best and did well. Since then, I've been doing better at being a lawyer, because it thoroughly captures my whole spirit. When I go home at night, I'm both relaxed and exhilarated.

The biggest thing, no matter who you are or where you are in your life, is to realize it's okay to fail. You can make a mistake or you can lose, and you don't need to stop there. It's only a step. You look at why you failed or why you lost and you learn from it, and you realize you're going to fail or lose less going forward. It builds up confidence when you fail, get back up, and take on the challenge again the next time.

Failure is part of life. What makes it a positive is when you can fail and you move on and attain another goal, or attempt it again. It's about not giving up.

Q: What advice would you give a new lawyer?

A: Find an area of law which is consistent with your passions in life. You'll find the days are more fulfilling than having to spend your time doing things where your heart isn't truly participating in the efforts you're putting forth.

If you're going to be a compassionate advocate, master the art of listening. Many advocates believe their position is the best and only one, so when they're in a deposition they're blind to everything outside their perspective. Instead, when you're meeting with opposing counsel, talking to people within the investigation, doing discovery of a witness, or anything involved in your case where someone else is talking, you need to stop and soak it up. Listen to every word possible. It's amazing what little gems pop up over the course of your patient listening.

Also, attention to detail is paramount. Every time you think you know the answer, presume you don't. Every time you think you've turned over every rock, keep looking for more rocks to turn over.

Young people who get into this business must have a sense of that social responsibility. Some do it for the money, and that's unfortunate, but inadvertently they still do well, because they're pointing out errors doctors made, or product defects that shouldn't have existed. It's a good specialty for those who have that sense of social justice in them and the desire to help people.

ACTION GUIDE

An easy reference guide to the advice and tips provided by Thomas Nathan

1) Find an Area of the Law Consistent with Your Passion in Life

You'll find the days are more fulfilling there than when you're doing things that don't make your heart truly participate in the efforts you're putting forth. Identify your passion, get into it, pay your dues, and then enjoy it.

2) Master the Art of Listening

Regarding anything involved in your case where someone else is talking, stop and soak it up. Listen to every word possible. It's amazing what little gems pop up over the course of your patient listening.

3) Pay Attention to the Details

Every time you think you know the answer, presume you don't. Every time you think you've turned over every rock, keep looking for more rocks to turn over.

4) Remember, You Work to Live, You Don't Live to Work

Cherish your spouse, family, and friends, and place them on the top of your priority list. You can practice law more effectively within the harmony of a whole life as opposed to the discord of an imbalanced one. Recognize what's truly important in life and set the right priorities for your time.

CHAPTER 6

Bruce Tizes

BIOGRAPHY

"We live in a highly legalistic society and some knowledge of the law is required for all well-rounded people. Whether it's perfected to the extent of a law degree is a subjective decision. But, no adult can function in America without a functional knowledge of the law."

~ Bruce Tizes

Bruce Tizes was born in New York City in 1960. He received his Bachelor of Science degree from the University of the State of New York in 1982 and his Doctor of Medicine degree two years later from The Chicago Medical School. After completing his two-year residency in Internal Medicine there, he moved on to Kings County Hospital, Brooklyn, New York, where he served as Chief Resident in the Ophthalmology Department.

While continuing his active medical career, primarily in emergency medicine, Tizes went back to school, earning his Juris Doctor degree in 1999 from Chicago's Northwestern University School of Law in 1999.

He has been an investor/trader for many years and, in addition to his professional career, has been actively involved in a broad range of activities, both in business and the arts. For example, he has served as executive producer of 11 films, from Three Days of Rain in 2003 (starring Peter Falk) to Chamaco in 2009 (starring Martin Sheen). His 12th film, Revenge of the Nerds III, is scheduled for release in 2017.

INTERVIEW

Q: Will you please introduce yourself?

A: My name is Bruce Randolph Tizes. I'm engaged in a variety of endeavors, including medicine, business, creative arts including filmmaking, health, and thinking about law.

My mother and grandmother were New York City public school teachers. My father was born in Romania, where almost all his siblings were killed during World War II. He eventually came to the United States in 1959. Until the day he died, he was exceptionally proud to be an American. I see the world, in large part, through his eyes.

Q: At what age did you start college?

A: I started at age 15. I finished college – that is, I was done with college – when I was 16. My medical degree was conferred when I was 23 years old.

Q: Did you pursue your M.D. first or your law degree first?

A: I attended medical school first, and I published my first scientific paper. I started working on it at about age 10. It was to be published at age 11 or 12 in The Journal of Geology. Then I published my second science-based paper, which was medical/legal, when I was about 13, in The Journal of Legal Medicine.

I'd say my interest in these things we call medicine and the law is both indivisible and has always been part of my general areas of interest as I look at the world around me.

Q: What kind of medicine do you practice?

A: I was formally trained in internal medicine and ophthalmology. I practiced emergency medicine from 1983 forward. So, the largest part of my life in medicine was spent practicing emergency medicine.

Q: Are you an independent person?

A: I was carefully taught at an early age to try to think independently and fundamentally. So, one of the few insights I can offer to your readers is to look for fundamental insights when looking at the world. Rules of thumb are disruptive. They obstruct one's thinking by occupying the terrain that ought to be occupied by a fundamental principle. Yes, so I hope I'm an independent thinker.

There are many things I know that I don't know, but I try for fundamental principles.

Q: How did starting college so young impact you?

A: Oh, I was fine. I was lucky. I took my first public course when I was 9 or 10 years old. I enrolled in a calculus course in Brooklyn College in the summer because it looked like fun. It wasn't necessarily fun, as it turned out. But, my social experience was fine. For whatever reason, I've always felt comfortable in my own skin, and so I never felt marginalized, despite a large age gap between my cohorts or peers.

Q: Was your family supportive?

A: My parents and maternal grandmother were quite supportive. In my household, at the dinner table one has to speak the lexicon of medicine and law and back up one's position by evidence. This is to say we've had a daily discourse of the matters at hand, and I was expected to defend my position.

Q: When did you first start thinking about a career in law?

A: We live in a highly legalistic society, so as far back as I can remember (perhaps from age two), I started thinking about the rules that bind us. I became aware of organizing principles by which we're governed. So, I thought about the law at the earliest opportunities.

The way the law had been studied up until the time of formalized education was by reading for the law. Whether you look backward to the Justinian code in ancient Rome or ancient French law or Hebrew law or so forth, one would study as an apprentice under a more experienced person.

In America, we moved away from reading for the law and developed a series of institutions of higher education which purport to teach it. So, if I could have read for the law alone and later found myself admitted to the practice (if I wanted to be admitted), I would've done it that way. But that doesn't exist any longer. So, I first thought about learning the law in the earliest part of childhood.

I had aspirations to attend law school and legal college. But, it was much later when I realized the constraints of professional and competitive associations were such that being admitted to practice law for all intents and purposes requires one to attend an APA accredited law school.

Q: When did you start law school?

A: I started law school in my late 30s, although I'd applied to law school once in my mid-20s, but was unable to attend.

I worked all night at King's County Hospital in Brooklyn, New York. When I drove up to meet with the higher academics at Cornell Law School, where I decided to attend, I had an appointment somewhere in mid-afternoon. After working the entire preceding day and night, then driving up and sitting in the admissions office, I fell asleep in a chair waiting for my interview. The high ranking person who awakened me commented that I might not be interested in Cornell if I fell asleep there. After I explained what had caused me to fall asleep, the interview went very well.

Q: Did you stop practicing medicine to pursue law?

A: I don't view the world in that way. I don't stop doing anything in particular once I've acquired it. I'm still interested in the subject matter, and I'm pushing to learn more. But, I never stopped medicine. I kept at it one way or another all during law school. My classmates were all full-time students, but I was also working.

Q: Why did you want to study law?

A: We live in a highly legalistic society and some knowledge of the law is required for all well-rounded people. Whether it's perfected to the extent of a law degree is a subjective decision. But, no adult can function in America without a functional knowledge of the law.

There are certainly events in my life that have been legalistic, but the attendance of law school is only for the purpose of being admitted to the practice of law. One can acquire all the knowledge one might want to freely acquire in the public domain. So, the attendance in law school is designed to allow me at some future time, should I choose, to form a practice.

The kind of law I'm interested in is the delivery of justice and arriving at just and equitable results. The members of our society who seldom receive justice are the poor and the excluded and the downtrodden. They're the same group I took care of in medicine and the same group by which we can judge as a society.

So, when you ask me what kind of law would I then interested in, it remains the same as it's always been. Eventually, I'll probably practice law in defense of people who are neglected in various senses.

I don't like to waste time. I prefer to direct my attention to places where there are needs. I view myself to be here of some service and to explore the boundaries of knowledge. Those whom I've always paid attention to the most, after my primary needs are met, are people who need a bit of help.

Q: What interests you most in law?

A: I like the little guy. I always stick up for the little guy against the big guy. I don't have any particular claim to importance that's any more or less important than anybody else's. If I'm lucky I'll find myself in a personal service to some people who seek my attention. That's it. It's nothing larger or grander than that.

Q: How would you suggest people approach law?

A: They should approach it with a high degree of skepticism and an even higher degree of respect for the series of knowledge nuggets that are embodied in the common law. The study of law may equally well be called the study of how we civilize the beast with little sympathy or empathy and live happily ever after. With that in mind, the study of law rises to the highest level of human accomplishment.

Q: How long have you had your law degree?

A: Approximately 16 years.

Q: How long have you practiced law?

A: I've never practiced law.

Q: Why haven't you?

A: We all use the law every day. I've never been retained by a client in a representative capacity such that the admission to the practice of law would have been required. I'm more of a practical person. So, my general sense is that I'd like to apply it fundamentally.

I do try to reach clear agreements with people. I'd rather resolve a dispute amicably while intentions are good than an adjudicated dispute when tempers are heated and emotional decision making has come to the fore.

Q: How important is administration and enforcement of existing laws?

A: You're touching on a tremendously important subject. I'm a reasonably educated, not particularly well-educated, citizen. But, I can't hold all the laws in my head. I can't even hold all the laws that apply to me in my head. I can't even hold the definitions or the names of the laws that apply to me in my daily existence in my head. So what we have is a colossal failure of the law to communicate its rules in a cogent and accessible format to its citizens. We have a tremendous failure.

Parenthetically, I'd be pleased to work on a book that goes through the law and reveals the ridiculous criminalization of Americans. We're all guilty of criminal, not only civil, violations on a daily basis that we have no idea about. This is all about the maintenance of an overt class of politicians whose main function is to engorge themselves at the expense of the working public.

Q: Where is the balance or the place where you have so many laws where an individual doesn't have any freedom anymore? Is there a balance between the two?

A: The obvious answer is we need the right number of laws – no more and no less.

It's as few as possible. A classic example is yelling "fire" in a movie theatre. In general, we have a right to free speech. We don't have a right to free speech in ways that have been curtailed by our laws. You don't have the right to yell "fire" in a movie theatre because the fear of risk in the people who hear it would be so high that they'll presumably disregard ordinary caution and stampede for the exits, causing a variety of problems or potential injuries.

If you're asking me about the essence of freedom in America, freedom has departed these shores. We're living in a nation-state in which there's an illusion of freedom at the most basic peer-to-peer level, and that freedom gradually diminishes as government focuses its attention on us.

Also, the different technologies available today that circumvent traditional common-law notions of privacy are so extreme as to make nothing private any longer. The combination of laws that are so plentiful and incomprehensible with the heavy hand of government force and the lack of privacy and technological infiltration in their lives is such that there's no freedom left to be had here.

Q: There are cultural laws that aren't necessarily coded laws. Which do you think are more powerful?

A: Things that are more local tend to have a larger application in a person's day-to-day activities. I suspect they develop in a larger fraction of time than intended. I'd guess when all is said and done the superstructure of society is much more consequential than the individual mores.

Q: So when looking at solutions, what motivates people to take actions that would make the world healthier?

A: The most powerful motivators are those that provide immediate return. We're a short-term oriented society, so we move a lot when we want reproductive opportunities, or food, or shelter, and we tend not to do well when investing our capital for long-term retirement plans. And that would be an ordinary example of needing to use the big computing device between our ears to overcome the short-term rewards of spending the money today.

For example, we have a lot of problems in the United States with food because, in part, sugar is so pleasant that we've developed an immediate reward for the consumption of the substance and it interferes with our capacity to maintain long-term beneficial outcomes. What motivates humans? The short answer is short-term sugar does.

Q: Can codified laws influence consumers' behaviors more to break short-term habits?

A: A law that prohibits the supply of a substance will drive the supply of that substance to less obvious suppliers. So, laws do have a consequential effect on the supply of things. Were we to make any law that prohibited the sale of alcohol to minors, we might see fewer automobile accidents involving alcohol in minors. And, we've done those kinds of things.

Were we to make a law that prohibits the sale of soft drinks in schools, we might see a marginal impact upon the obesity of teenagers and so on.

I'm a free market person, so I wouldn't make nearly anything illegal. I'd simply educate and make available adequate resources so people can reach their own conclusions.

We're living in difficult times today, and we're moving from public laws to private laws, from contract law to private law. As we develop more environments that are run by hybrid entities and corporations, such as Mars launches and moon launches, which will be run with the supervision of particular corporations, those corporations will operate with the absolute force of law.

You might ask the question of what copyright law is in the context of Google. Of what virtue of holding and not holding a copyright or a trademark is there if Google has a series of principles they follow internally in adjudicating a dispute? We're moving quickly and don't know where we're headed.

I've given you a series of principles that seem reasonable. One is that we look for fundamental truths. Another is that we know some "what's" and few "why's." The third is to be of some humble service to people who seek you out.

The law is important. I'm proud of the law I participate in, but the way it's implemented currently in America is profoundly unfair.

People always help their self-interest. They vote what they do for their tribal interests, and they vote for the red or the blue team and they're not even sure why they're a member of that team except that their father or mother was once a member.

Q: Do you think empathy is more important than law?

A: You can derive many principles in the law from things like private property rights. If you combine private property with empathy you get almost all of it. You get most of what we've learned in those two baskets.

I have a risk-based approach to my calculations, and I'm always looking at what the return on risk is, to the best of my ability to understand risk. I do it in medicine, law, or anything else. The risk to us is that we become callous and unfeeling creatures to our detriment – and to the detriment of others.

The benefit to us is to become more humane and that's my fondest desire. I imagine a time when everyone has food and shelter and is able to perfect their own interests and those of the people they hold most dear or compelling. Maybe we are headed that way; I hope we are headed that way.

Q: Do you have any final words of advice for law students?

A: The law is both one of the most remarkable accomplishments of man, and insufficient for the purpose to which it is put. It is in the application of honorable systematic legal principles that fundamental justice is found or disregarded. Unitarian Minister Theodore Parker insightfully said in 1853: "I do not pretend to understand the moral universe. The arc is a long one. My eye reaches but little ways. I cannot calculate the curve and complete the figure by experience of sight. I can divine it by conscience. And from what I see I am sure it bends toward justice." My advice to students of law is related – apply yourself creatively in service to a law that bends toward justice.

RESOURCES

Resources for Law Students and New Attorneys

WEB RESOURCES

American Association of Law Libraries

http://www.aallnet.org/default.aspx

The American Association of Law Libraries was founded in 1906 to promote and enhance the value of law libraries to the legal and public communities, to foster the profession of law librarianship, and to provide leadership in the field of legal information. With nearly 5,000 members, the Association represents law librarians and related professionals who are affiliated with a wide range of institutions: law firms; law schools; corporate legal departments; courts; and local, state, and federal government agencies. The American Association of Law Libraries advances the profession of law librarianship and supports the professional growth of its members through leadership and advocacy in the field of legal information and information policy.

American Bar Association

https://www.americanbar.org/groups/lawyer_assistance/articles_and_info/law_student_resources.html

The American Bar Association is one of the world's largest voluntary professional organizations, with over 400,000 members and more than 3,500 entities. It is committed to doing what only a national association of attorneys can do: serving our members, improving the legal profession, eliminating bias and enhancing diversity, and advancing the rule of law throughout the United States and around the world.

Founded in 1878, the ABA is committed to supporting the legal profession with practical resources for legal professionals while improving the administration of justice, accrediting law schools, establishing model ethical codes, and more. Membership is open to lawyers, law students, and others interested in the law and the legal profession.

Bloomberg Law

https://www.bna.com/law-student-resources/

Our products provide legal, tax, compliance, government affairs and government contracting professionals with critical information, practical guidance and workflow solutions. We leverage leading technology and a global network of experts to deliver a unique combination of news and authoritative analysis, comprehensive research solutions, innovative practice tools, and proprietary business data and analytics. Bloomberg BNA is an affiliate of Bloomberg L.P., the global business, financial information and news leader.

Our flagship products – Bloomberg Law®, Bloomberg Tax and Bloomberg Government® – are fully integrated research solutions that combine trusted news and expert analysis with comprehensive market data, primary source material and cutting-edge technologies. These integrated solutions enable professionals to make more informed decisions, provide insightful guidance, grow their businesses and streamline their work.

Find Law

http://www.findlaw.com/

FindLaw, a part of Thomson Reuters, is a pioneer and innovator in marketing solutions for law firms, online legal information and services for lawyers, businesses, and individuals.

The great innovations of Silicon Valley so often start with two guys in a garage. Apple, HP, and countless start-ups owe their beginnings to a few people with a good idea, a place to work -- and little more. We are no different. FindLaw began with two attorneys in an apartment, with an idea. In 1995, FindLaw's founders compiled a list of online resources for a group of law librarians in Northern California. The response to this idea was so positive they decided to post the information on the Internet. FindLaw was born.

Google Scholar

https://scholar.google.com/

Google Scholar provides a simple way to broadly search for scholarly literature. From one place, you can search across many disciplines and sources: articles, theses, books, abstracts and court opinions, from academic publishers, professional societies, online repositories, universities and other web sites. Google Scholar helps you find relevant work across the world of scholarly research.

Justia

https://www.justia.com/

Based in the heart of Silicon Valley, Justia's mission is to advance the availability of legal resources for the benefit of society. We are especially focused on making primary legal materials and community resources free and easy to find on the Internet. The company provides Internet users with free case law, codes, regulations, legal articles and legal blog and twitterer databases, as well as additional community resources. Justia works with educational, public interest and other socially focused organizations to bring legal and consumer information to the online community.

Law.com

http://www.law.com

Law.com is the premier source for trusted and timely legal news and analysis. Subscribers to the site can access stories from across ALM's national and regional publications, with the opportunity to view news by practice area. Each practice area offers a rich selection of articles, curated by ALM's expert editorial team. In addition, Law.com features views from leading voices in the legal field through the Law.com Contributor Network.

The National LGBT Bar Association

https://lgbtbar.org/what-we-do/law-student-resources/

The National LGBT Bar Association boasts the largest group of lesbian, gay, bisexual and transgender law students in the country. As such, the LGBT Bar is a tremendous resource for law students. The LGBT Bar, along with its law student division, the Law Student Congress, seeks to connect LGBT students and student organizations around the country. The LGBT Bar offers an online community platform that allows law students to interact not only with other law students from across the country, but also lawyers, judges and other legal professionals, activists, and affiliated lesbian, gay, bisexual, and transgender legal organizations. Law student members of the bar also get special discounts, including reduced rates for the annual Lavender Law Conference.

The Public Library of Law

http://www.plol.org

Searching the Web is easy. Why should searching the law be any different? That's why Fastcase has created the Public Library of Law -- to make it easy to find the law online. PLoL is one of the largest free law libraries in the world, because we assemble law available for free scattered across many different sites -- all in one place. PLoL is the best starting place to find law on the Web.

Sandra Day O'Connor College of Law

http://www.law.asu.edu/

The Sandra Day O'Connor College of Law is pioneering a new model for 21st century legal education, one that reinvents the modern law school as not just an institution that trains lawyers, but as a multifaceted legal studies center that engages in developing solutions to the world's global challenges and that seeks to educate a broad cross-section of contemporary society.

Steps to Becoming a Lawyer

http://www.lawyeredu.org/

Lawyeredu.org was created as an effort to encourage more people to consider a career in law. Today more than ever before, lawyers are needed in a variety of specialties that have arisen due to recent changes in technology, foreign and domestic policy, and health care. If you are in the process of fulfilling specific requirements on becoming a lawyer or attorney please be sure to view our step by step process pages by state here.

Ten Things to Know Before Law School

www.ingredientsofoutliers.com

In anticipation of our book release, Outliers in Law, we contacted a seasoned attorney who gave us the 411 on law school, including what you need to know before you go and how to thrive once you are there. We decided to split his advice into two different posts. His first set of tips are things you need to consider before even entering law school. The next set of tips will focus on things you need to know before you graduate law school, and enter a career as an attorney.

Thirteen Things to Know Before You Graduate Law School
www.ingredientsofoutliers.com

In light of our book release, Outliers in Law, we asked one of our favorite attorneys to give us the 411 on law school: what you need to know before you go and how to thrive once you are there. Having practiced law for 10 years now, we knew he would have a great perspective on school and his career, but we had no idea he would give 23 priceless tips.

Top 40 Law YouTube Channels Every Lawyer Must Follow
https://blog.feedspot.com/law_youtube_channels/

Feedspot's list of Law YouTube channels ranked by popularity.

Top 100 Legal Blogs Every Lawyer and Law Student Must Follow
https://blog.feedspot.com/legal_law_blogs/

The Best Legal blogs from thousands of top Legal blogs in our index using search and social metrics. Data will be refreshed once a week.

U.S. News and World Report Best Law Schools:
http://gradschools.usnews.rankingsandreviews.com/best-graduate-schools/top-law-schools

The U.S. News rankings of 198 law schools fully accredited by the American Bar Association are based on a weighted average of the 12 measures of quality described below. Data were collected in fall 2014 and early 2015. Specialty rankings are based solely on nominations by legal educators at peer institutions.

U.S. Supreme Court
http://www.supremecourt.gov/

The Supreme Court consists of the Chief Justice of the United States and such number of Associate Justices as may be fixed by Congress.

The number of Associate Justices is currently fixed at eight (28 U. S. C. §1). Power to nominate the Justices is vested in the President of the United States, and appointments are made with the advice and consent of the Senate. Article III, §1, of the Constitution further provides that "[t]he Judges, both of the supreme and inferior Courts, shall hold their Offices during good Behaviour, and shall, at stated Times, receive for their Services, a Compensation, which shall not be diminished during their Continuance in Office."

BOOKS

Constitutional Law: Principles and Policies

by Erwin Chemerinsky

http://a.co/d/dsoSeld

Relied on by students, professors, and practitioners, this popular treatise clearly states the law and identifies the underlying policy issues in each area of constitutional law. Thorough coverage of the topic makes it appropriate for both beginning and advanced courses.

Expert Learning for Law Students

by Michael Hunter Schwartz

http://a.co/d/3EWKUoJ

This book is designed to help law students build the analytical skills necessary to succeed in law school, on the bar exam, and in law practice. It reveals how successful law students and lawyers plan, monitor, and implement their work and provides detailed guidance regarding individual student personality types and learning styles. The accompanying workbook includes questions and exercises to assist students in practicing the concepts explained in the text.

Global Legal Pluralism: A Jurisprudence of Law Beyond Borders

by Paul Schiff Berman

http://a.co/d/ip3AJeJ

We live in a world of legal pluralism, where a single act or actor is potentially regulated by multiple legal or quasi-legal regimes imposed by state, substate, transnational, supranational and nonstate communities. Navigating these spheres of complex overlapping legal authority is confusing and we cannot expect territorial borders to solve all these problems. At the same time, those hoping to create one universal set of legal rules are also likely to be disappointed by the sheer variety of human communities and interests. Instead, we need an alternative jurisprudence, one that seeks to create or preserve spaces for productive interaction among multiple, overlapping legal systems by developing procedural mechanisms, institutions and practices that aim to manage, without eliminating, the legal pluralism we see around us. Global Legal Pluralism provides a broad synthesis across a variety of legal doctrines and academic disciplines and offers a novel conceptualization of law and globalization.

Law School Confidential: A Complete Guide to the Law School Experience: For Students, by Students

by Robert H. Miller

http://a.co/d/aeQtzUv

Written by students, for students, this has been the "must-have" guide for anyone thinking about, applying to, or attending law school for more than a decade. And now, in this newly revised third edition, it's more valuable than ever.

This isn't the advice of graying professors or battle-scarred practitioners long removed from law school. Robert H. Miller has assembled a blue-ribbon panel of recent graduates from across the country to offer realistic and informative firsthand advice about what law school is really like.

The Nature of the Judicial Process

Benjamin N. Cardozo et al.

http://a.co/d/bWhqArp

Judges don't discover the law, they create it. Cardozo (1870-1938) offered the world a candid and self-conscious study of how judges decide law – they are law-makers and not just law-appliers, he knew – drawn from his insights on the bench, in a way that no judge had before. Asked "What is it that I do when I decide a case? To what sources of information do I appeal for guidance?" Cardozo answered in timeless prose. This book is still read today by lawyers and judges, law students and scholars, historians and political scientists, and philosophers – anyone interested in how judges really think and the many decisional tools they employ. Already famous at the time for his trenchant and fluid opinions as a Justice on New York's highest court (he is still studied on questions of torts, contracts, and business law), and later a Justice of the U.S. Supreme Court, Cardozo filled the lecture hall at Yale when he finally answered the frank query into what judges do and how they do it. The lectures became a landmark book and a source for all other studies of the ways of a judge.

The Pre-Writing Handbook for Law Students: A Step-by-Step Guide

by Laura P. Graham, Miriam E. Felsenburg

http://a.co/d/hfGNQ59

Intended primarily for use in the first few weeks of the first-semester legal writing course, this guide takes a systematic approach to the process of preparing to write legal memos, briefs, and other documents. It is designed to help students focus on and become competent in the process of legal analysis that precedes their work on a written product.

The Handbook is uniquely designed to help students gauge their own progress as they work through the pre-writing process. The confidence students will gain from engaging in the pre-writing process as outlined will translate into a smoother, more effective writing process and a better written product.

Scholarly Writing for Law Students: Seminar Papers, Law Review Notes & Law Review Comp Papers

by Elizabeth Fajans, Mary Falk

http://a.co/d/hDtA02q

This book fills an important niche in legal-writing literature by teaching law students how to write scholarly papers for seminars, law reviews, and law-review competitions and how to have their work recognized. It helps novices and more experienced scholars alike to write papers with a minimum of anxiety and a maximum of creativity. Employing a process theory of writing, the text first describes the enterprise of scholarly writing and then discusses techniques for brainstorming topics and theses, researching, drafting, and revising for substance and style. It covers both traditional doctrinal topics and newer areas like empirical studies.

There are also chapters on footnotes, avoiding plagiarism, law review practice, and dissemination of student work through publication and submission to national writing competitions. Appendices provide a sample law-review competition paper, answers to in-text exercises, sample syllabi for scholarly writing courses, and a rubric for evaluating and editing scholarly papers and articles.

What Every Law Student Really Needs to Know: An Introduction to the Study of Law

by Tracey George

http://a.co/d/i3pGH6C

This brief book is designed to prepare students for their first year of law school, thereby decreasing their anxiety and increasing their chances of achieving academic success. Also appropriate for non-J.D. students, including LLM students from foreign countries and graduate students outside law school.

PODCASTS

ABA Law Student Podcast

https://legaltalknetwork.com/podcasts/aba-law-student-podcast/

Presented by the American Bar Association's Law Student Division, the ABA Law Student Podcast covers issues that affect law students, law schools, and recent grads. From finals and graduation to the bar exam and finding a job, this show is your trusted resource for the next big step.

Best Podcasts for Law Students

https://www.thoughtco.com/best-podcasts-for-law-students-2154998

Blogs can be helpful for new law students, but many people enjoy listening to podcasts as well. Podcasts can be a great way to get information and give your very tired eyes a break from reading online. To help you update your podcast subscriptions, here is a list of some of the best podcasts for law students.

Listen Up, Law Students: These Podcasts Could Help You Study https://www.theguardian.com

Studying law will entail endless hours of reading case law and textbooks, but there's no reason to limit your learning to sitting at a desk. Podcasts are an excellent way of expanding your knowledge, whether you're in the library or strolling to the pub. Here's our list of some of the most interesting and helpful podcasts for law undergraduates.

Podcasts for Law Students
https://www.survivelaw.com/single-post/2233-podcasts-for-law-students

This is a list of podcasts recommended by Survive Law for being entertaining, informative or engaging. Sometimes even all three. Listening to just one episode of each of these podcasts a week will take you just over two and a half hours (this week's episodes add up to 199 minutes). And at the end of it you'll know more about the latest in the law, kooky crime stories and the ins and outs of the economy than you ever have. Or at least more than you did before.

Top Legal Podcasts
https://www.filevine.com/blog/top-legal-podcasts/

With the growing popularity of podcasts, an entire genre of law-related podcasts have sprung up to provide entertainment, information, and education in the area of law. Podcasts have become a valuable resource for lawyers to stay up-to-date on legal trends, cases, and laws, as well as find information on running a successful firm.

Top Podcasts for Law Students
https://lawschooltoolbox.com/top-podcasts-for-law-students/

Podcasts are not only a super convenient way to make your commute fly by, but also a great method to keep up with the law and everything involving it. In case you're not sure where to start or want some new podcast suggestions, The Law School Toolbox reviewed a few well-known legal podcasts.

CONCLUSION

It's my sincere hope that these amazing outliers motivate you as much as they did me. Their stories reveal what may not have been apparent from the perspective of an outsider, who may have thought that, given their successes, their paths were straight and easy. To hear their stories about how they faced setbacks and adapted to adversity, told in such an honest and straightforward manner, is both sobering and inspiring.

What is so transparent is that none of these professionals had anything simply handed to them. They all fought hard for their accomplishments and were ultimately successful through perseverance, humility and by following their passion. They were not perfect nor were they on a straight trajectory. No one is.

What their stories illustrate is that all of us can aspire to greatness and accomplish anything we're passionate about, as long as we persevere and accept some failures along the way. Maybe after passion, the most important attribute is to be fearless as it relates to failure. In other words, accept the fact that you'll likely fail your way to success because, at the end of the day – if it were easy, everyone would do it, and success would be no accomplishment at all.

The Action Guides highlight nuggets from each outlier's path to success, and the Resource Guides provide some additional sources of information.

You now have everything you need: six great mentors, a path to follow, and some additional resources to help you along the way. What are you waiting for? Go out and accomplish your most amazing future, and join the ranks of the outliers!

I will end this as I ended the other books in the series with a quote from Mark Twain:

Twenty years from now you will be more disappointed by the things that you didn't do than by the ones you did do. So throw off the bowlines. Sail away from the safe harbor. Catch the trade winds in your sails. Explore. Dream. Discover.

FOLLOW THE OUTLIER MOVEMENT

www.facebook.com/readingredientsofoutliers

www.twitter.com/JohnShufeldt

ingredientsofoutliers@gmail.com

ADDITIONAL WORKS BY DR. JOHN SHUFELDT

The Outlier Series

Ingredients of Outliers: A Recipe for Personal Achievement
June 2013

Ingredients of Young Outliers: Achieving Your Most Amazing Future
March 2014

Ingredients of Outliers: Women Game Changers
January 2015

Outliers in Medicine
April 2015

LeadershipYOU: Your Future Starts With You
April 2017

You Economy: Inspiring Your Inner Entrepreneur
March 2018

Made in the USA
Monee, IL
04 November 2026

67379685R00066